'Brilliant! Tough questions deserve clear and convincing answers. This is "state of the art" apologetics that needs no apology. Amy's fascinating, wise and informative comments impressively counter much of the superficial and frequently unchallenged debunking of the Bible that we meet everywhere today, e.g. in lightweight journalism, TV documentaries and blockbuster novels like *The Da Vinci Code*. A must-read for every armchair critic, historian and philosopher. User-friendly and great fun too!'
Greg Haslam,
Minister, Westminster Chapel, London

'This superb book tackles ten difficult questions about the Bible with honesty, integrity and conviction. It will be invaluable to anyone grappling with these questions.'
J. John,
Evangelist, The Philo Trust, Rickmansworth

'Amy Orr-Ewing is emerging as one of the finest young Christian communicators of our day. This excellent book confronts ten difficult questions about the Bible with honesty and conviction. It will be invaluable to anyone wrestling with these questions, or trying to help others who wrestle with them.'
Alister McGrath,
Professor of Historical Theology, Oxford University.
Director, Oxford Centre for Evangelism and Apologetics

The Zacharias Trust is the European Office of Ravi Zacharias International Ministries. It was founded to come alongside the church to help reach an increasingly secular Europe. Its vision is to engage with the questions of both sceptics and believers by offering an apologetic that makes sense to both heart and mind. Its services include providing its, and training for Christian to sceptics. For more information site at www.zactrust.org.

D1424323

WHY TRUST THE BIBLE?

ANSWERS TO 10 TOUGH QUESTIONS
AMY ORR-EWING

INTER-VARSITY PRESS
38 De Montfort Street, Leicester LE1 7GP, England
Email: ivp@uccf.org.uk
Website: www.ivpbooks.com

First published 2005

British Library Cataloguing in Publication Data
A catalogue record for this book is available from the British Library.

ISBN-13: 978-0-85111-993-9
ISBN-10: 0-85111-993-X

Set in Dante 10.5/13pt
Typeset in Great Britain by CRB Associates, Reepham, Norfolk
Printed and bound in Great Britain by Creative Print and Design (Wales),
Ebbw Vale

*Inter-Varsity Press is the publishing division of the Universities and
Colleges Christian Fellowship (formerly the Inter-Varsity Fellowship),
a student movement linking Christian Unions in universities and
colleges throughout Great Britain, and a member movement of the
International Fellowship of Evangelical Students. For more information
about local and national activities write to UCCF, 38 De Montfort Street,
Leicester LE1 7GP, email us at email@uccf.org.uk, or visit the UCCF
website at www.uccf.org.uk.*

Contents

Foreword

I have travelled the globe for over thirty years, speaking in academic settings throughout Europe and the East. In many of these venues I have encountered the much-heralded belief of postmodernism that scepticism on ultimate matters is the law by which we must live. The diminishing value of words and the dismissal of Truth as a category, on metaphysical issues, is popular and celebrated. All is relative.

But the words of Winston Churchill still haunt: 'In time of war, when truth is so precious, it must be attended by a bodyguard of lies.' He made that remark in the context of intelligence and counter-intelligence efforts during the Second World War.

I believe this surrender of truth is the benchmark of our culture's greatest crisis, for it restricts meaningful dialogue on questions of the soul. Those who castigate truth go further. They label anyone who holds to the possibility of truth as one who 'believes', implying thereby that the content that is held to be true is 'mere belief'. At the same time, they themselves can end up believing anything at all, and that belief is considered plausible merely because it is hostile to truth. The 'war' declared on truth and the devaluing of words is a self-defeating pursuit unless their opponents make true claims and speak meaningful words.

In life our methods call our bluff when we are confronted with the undeniable relationship between truth and living. For instance, in a Canadian survey among young people, the majority stated that their greatest longing in life was to find someone they could believe in.

Yet the question remains, *How do we arrive at the truth?* For the Christian, the starting point is God, and who he has revealed himself to be in the Bible. He is the eternally existent one, the absolute, from whom we draw all definitions for life's purpose and destiny. This God, who is the source of all truth, has so framed this world and our minds that the laws of reason and logic lead us to the certainty and knowledge of his being.

There is absolutely no doubt that the Christian message stands or falls upon the authenticity or spuriousness of the Bible. Knowing it to be God's Word, millions across history have staked their lives upon it. Destiny-defining trust has been placed in it. Graveside hope has been based upon it. Extraordinary good has been spread because of it. The charters of nations have been built upon it. With equal intensity others have sought to expel it, and wrong-headed zeal has caused untold evil in its name. There is no book in history that has been so studied, so used, and so abused as the Holy Bible.

Having this Book as a mirror for life and a map for the soul is the most profound authority we can have in life. Its truths and its truthfulness have been demonstrated across history. Often when I see an unyielding questioner claiming that God has not given us enough evidence, I wonder if the real problem is the veiled restlessness of a life that lives in doubt because of deeper existential questions. The struggle in our time is posed as one of the intellect, in the assertion that truth is unknowable. But that may be only a veneer for the real struggle, which is that of the heart.

When Pilate asked Jesus the question, 'What is truth?', Jesus answered him with a categorical response. In effect, Jesus was asking Pilate if his was a genuine question or purely an academic one. Jesus was not merely checking on Pilate's sincerity. He was opening up Pilate's heart to himself, to reveal to Pilate his unwillingness to deal with the implications of Jesus' answer. 'They who are on the side of truth, listen to me,' he said. *Intent* in the pursuit of truth is prior to content, or to the availability of it. The author George Macdonald once said, 'To give truth to him who loves it not is only to give him more plentiful reasons for misinterpretation.'

Jesus on numerous occasions harked back to the word of Scripture and promised that he would reveal his truth so that we might have it in written form. Scripture is the revelation of God, by Jesus' own attestation. Is there truth for all of us within its pages or is it only for those with superstitious and unsuspecting minds? Is the Bible mere fantasy, or is it fantastically true? Is this indeed the Word from God to us, or is it the fraudulent work of a few human beings, claiming divine superintendence?

These are the hard questions that my colleague Amy Orr-Ewing lays before us. Her own search for answers led her to Oxford University where she diligently pursued her academic discipline in the study of the New Testament. She knew well that it was not to be a cakewalk. She studied under those who forced her to ask the daunting and discomforting questions and face the challenge head-on. Her accomplishment was rewarded with recognized honour. I first met Amy and her husband, Frog, several years ago. It did not take long, while listening to her intense conviction and her tender heart, to know the seriousness of her pursuit of truth. After she finished her studies I was so delighted when she joined our team which works in defence of the Christian faith all over the world.

The subject matter here is truly a reflection of Amy's life and her gifts. She has faced the toughest audiences on the global scene, and when she is finished with her presentations, even the strident sceptic responds with respect for the integrity of her defence. In her many conversations and university forums, she engages questioners with truth, clarity, humility and genuine joy. She recognizes that the deepest longings of the human heart are often not explored because the intellectual questions appear as impassable roadblocks. The words of Churchill are true: 'Men stumble over the truth from time to time, but most pick themselves up and hurry off as if nothing happened.' Thankfully, in *Why Trust the Bible?* difficult questions are heard, and we are invited to slow down, and to consider the answers and our heart's true search. Nothing is more defining for all of life than to ask the question: 'Has God spoken and can we know that truth?' Then perhaps in turn, like the prophet Jeremiah, we may hear God's gracious response to us: 'Call to me and I will answer you and tell you great and unsearchable things you do not know' (Jeremiah 33:3). This book is an invaluable guide in directing us to know that call and to hear the response.

Dr Ravi Zacharias
March 2005
President of Ravi Zacharias Ministries

Introduction

In some countries of the world the book we are discussing here is contraband. Smuggling operations exist with the sole aim of getting Bibles secretly across closed borders and into the hands of those who want to read them. I will never forget getting off a train in the middle of China at four o'clock one morning and making my way to a rendezvous with three Chinese church leaders. A team of us were delivering bags filled with Bibles which were to be distributed amongst the churches further north. When our Chinese friends unzipped the bags and looked inside the tears began to flow down their cheeks. These books were so precious to them that they were prepared to risk imprisonment and persecution in order to get hold of them. I found it intriguing that the Bible should inspire such sacrifice and courage in the hearts of those who want to read it.

But why is the world's best-selling book rubbished by so many? Have you ever had the experience of someone turning to you and saying, 'You don't honestly believe all that stuff, do you?' I remember desperately searching for something credible to say when a friend came straight out and asked me, 'Noah's ark – do you believe in that?' I managed a feeble 'Yes' which was met with scorn and laughter by the group I was eating with. I'm sure many of us can identify both with being asked questions about the Bible and with asking them ourselves. After that early experience of finding myself speechless, I became determined to look for answers that would satisfy. Would the Bible really stand up to tough questioning?

That is what this book is all about. Many good Christian books have been written with the aim of giving clear answers to the questions which sceptics often ask about the Christian faith. Questions like 'Why is there suffering in the world if there is a God of love?' or 'Hasn't science proved that there is no God?' or 'What about all the other religions?' In these books there is usually a question along the lines of 'Can we really trust the Bible?' While the answers given are extremely valuable, I have found that all sorts of questions are raised about the Bible – each of which deserves a good answer in and of itself. That is what I am trying to do in this book. I have taken the ten questions about the Bible which have been asked most frequently in my experience and have attempted to look for some answers. Most of the answers offered here have been used in a simplified form in real-life conversations, although each chapter will also be looking for the bigger ideas behind the questions and placing the answers in a broader context.

My search for answers led me to study theology at University. But in my wildest dreams as a student at Oxford I never thought that one day I might have to defend my Christian faith before the dons of the University. That is, not until February of my final year. I was reading Theology at Christ Church, preparing for finals, when one night I dreamed that I would be viva-ed for my degree! A 'viva voce' is an oral examination which involves appearing before a panel of examiners and defending what you have written in your finals exams. This particular form of torture is usually reserved for examining doctorates. But sure enough, a couple of weeks after my degree was finished, towards the end of June, I received a phone call letting me know that I was required to appear before the theology faculty so that I could 'answer a few questions'. The date of the viva voce happened to be the day before my wedding! During my interview with these professors I was asked a number of questions about my Christian convictions. But one of them stands out, and I remember it as clearly as if it happened yesterday: 'You don't honestly mean to tell us that you think Jesus actually said the words recorded in the Gospels, or, for that matter, that the events recorded in the Bible really took place?'

My first impulse was to reply by asking, 'On what basis do you assume out of hand that Jesus did *not* say those words?' The astounding prejudice demonstrated here by highly intelligent people draws our attention to the scepticism with which the Bible is treated by many people in all walks of life. A conviction that the Bible must be wrong, held by those at the highest level of academic excellence, seems, in turn, to have been embraced at a popular level by many people who have barely glanced at the Bible, but who feel sure that it is not to be trusted.

My viva became the first of many occasions when I have been involved in defending the intellectual credibility of the Bible and, indeed, of the Christian faith, in different settings. As I go around with the Zacharias Trust and answer questions about the Christian message, I find that again and again many questions are asked specifically about the Bible. In our culture, which many call 'postmodern', the experts tell us that people are not interested in truth any more and are certainly not interested in authoritative texts like the Bible. And yet, time and time again, questions about the Bible come up in the course of my work with the Trust.

Initially I was surprised by many of the questions that were articulated. They were less about facts and evidence and more about ethics and interpretation. The questions of today seem to contain nuances of pluralism and postmodernism. All the questions dealt with in this book have been posed to me by non-Christians on many occasions.

After six years of working in the field of Christian apologetics, I have become convinced that if we are able to sensibly answer the concerns of the truth-seekers we come across, many will be brought to faith in Jesus Christ. For this reason, in this book I want to address the ten questions I am most commonly asked about the Bible.

Amy Orr-Ewing

Dedication
For Frog my husband and best friend

There are so many people that I would like to thank for supporting me and helping me with this project. My wonderful assistant Hanni Seddon, Sandra Byatt, Eleanor Trotter and editors at IVP, my colleagues in the RZIM family and my church, All Saints Peckham. Thank-you to Michael and Anne Ramsden for long-standing friendship, to Tim and Vanessa Norman for the use of their house whilst writing and to J. John and Killy for encouragement and inspiration. Thank-you too to Ravi and Margie Zacharias for believing in me. Thank-you to my sister Antje and brother-in-law Simon – you have constantly supported and been there for me. Finally, I would like to thank my parents Hartmut and Jane Kopsch who have inspired me over many years to love God and his word.

1 Isn't it all a matter of interpretation?

When it comes to talking about the Bible, people have all kinds of questions and suspicions. Often the picture in the mind's eye is of some strangely incoherent mystical writings which may be frightening. There is also a common perception that religious people use the Bible to shore up their own causes, that it is interpreted and used to mean whatever a particular group feels. This kind of statement may take the form of, 'You just make the Bible mean what you want it to mean! How can you expect me to take it seriously?' I have experienced this question coming in slightly different forms over the years. On one occasion I was talking to a fellow traveller at an airport. She had just finished a book which, she explained, claimed that Jesus married Mary Magdalene and ended up living happily ever after in Mesopotamia. Another friend of mine had read the same book and had drawn completely different conclusions from it. When I mentioned this, my fellow traveller was not at all surprised. As the conversation progressed, it became clear that the historical source material was not really important to her. This new book that she had enjoyed and the differing conclusions drawn from it by intelligent people just went to show that there are many interpretations of any text. This was then extended to apply to the Bible and the events it records. Meaning could not really be fixed – there is just a sea of valid opinions and no one 'reality' is to be found amongst them all.

The big issue behind the increasing numbers of questions about meaning and interpretation is the question of whether words and texts can have any inherent meaning at all. Does it all just come down to a matter of opinion? Is every interpretation equally valid? Can this text actually speak to me or do I make it mean what I want? This was powerfully communicated to my husband Francis (nicknamed Frog) a few years ago. He is a vicar and had taken a friend's wedding. After the church service we were sitting at a beautiful reception around a round table. I was talking to the young man sitting next to me and my husband was sitting next to the young man's girlfriend. As we began to talk, the man stopped in mid sentence and suddenly blurted out an apology – he said he found that, for some reason, he couldn't lie to me, and explained that before coming to the wedding he and his girlfriend had decided to swap lives. He was a wealthy management consultant and she was an artist. They had wanted to see if people treated them differently according to their status, and so they pretended to have each other's jobs. As we talked about why he might be uncomfortable about lying to me and other spiritual things, we looked over at our partners and he said, 'I wonder if my girlfriend has managed to hoodwink your husband . . . ' I silently prayed. After the wedding Frog explained to me that the young woman had also found herself unable to lie to him. They had also begun to talk about God and at one point she had said, 'The reason I am not a Christian is that I am studying English Literature, and I don't believe that there is a Transcendental Signified, and so I can make the Bible mean whatever I want it to mean.' Frog asked her to clarify, and she explained that she believed that words have no actual meaning – a word on a page or a word being heard only has the meaning that a reader or a hearer gives it. It does not itself carry any ultimate meaning because there is no God (Transcend-ental Signified) to give ultimate meaning to words. My husband looked at her and said: 'If that is the case – if words have no meaning except the meaning of the listener or reader – is it OK with you if I take what you have just said to mean, "I believe in Jesus and I am a Christian"?' At that moment she looked a little worried. She realized that her argument failed its own test. The standards by which she was judging the Bible were standards that her own thinking could not measure up to.

This issue of whether words have any meaning is incredibly important as we look at the Christian faith and as we offer the source materials about the life of Jesus – the New Testament Gospels – to our friends who do not believe in him. If the Bible only means what we make it mean, there is no point in reading it to discover anything about God.

Why do people believe that, when it comes to the Bible, everything is a matter of interpretation? It may help us to answer this question if we can understand where these ideas about interpretation and meaning come from.

The idea that there is no ultimate meaning in any text has become extremely powerful in our current postmodern context, and it has enormous implications for any communication about the gospel. One literary theorist writes:

> literature ... by refusing to assign a 'secret', an ultimate meaning, to the text (and to the world as text), liberates what may be called an anti-theological activity, an activity that is truly revolutionary since to refuse to fix meaning is, in the end, to refuse God ... [1]

Of course, this echoes the strangely prophetic words of the philosopher Friedrich Nietzsche: 'We cannot get rid of God until we get rid of grammar.'[2] This idea is later echoed by the atheist Bertrand Russell: 'Everyday language embodies the metaphysics of the Stone Age.'[3] The desire to liberate the human being from the constraint of a God is powerfully linked in with this issue of language and meaning.

Language as a game

There is sometimes a playfulness and whimsical quality about the approach of those who would seek to question the possibility of ultimate meaning in language. The philosopher Ludwig Wittgenstein (1889–1951) was an important influence in this field. He asserted that each use of language occurs within a separate and apparently self-contained system with its own rules. This means that any use of language would be similar to playing a game. We would need awareness of the rules of the game and a sense of the significance of terms in order to use the language. 'Each use of language constitutes a separate "language game" and various games have very little to do with one another.'[4]

Wittgenstein explicitly abandoned any concept of truth as correspondence with reality, and instead he characterized it as a function of language. This means that no statement or proposition can be limited to a single meaning – its meaning is completely dependent on context. And so all attempts at discovering truth or meaning are trapped by the language game in which they appear. When applied to the Bible, this means that the context of the reader is everything – context completely determines the interpretation of the text. It would be impossible to posit any unifying meaning which could be received by multiple cultures, languages, situations or 'games'.

We see this position argued for in many contexts today – admittedly, with less sophistication than Wittgenstein displayed, but the influence of his idea is visible. A statement like 'That was relevant then, but the Bible was written thousands of years ago' comes from the same point of view as Wittgenstein's. Of course, the Christian is in agreement that the context of any text is important for its interpretation. However, this does not mean that the same text cannot convey meaning outside of its original setting. If that were the case, it would apply to Wittgenstein's ideas themselves, which would have no relevance today. Appealing as that argument might be, Christians nevertheless still have to engage with these ideas, in the same way as we ask the Bible's detractors to honestly look at the New Testament with an open mind.

No universal world-view

Following on from this contextualization of meaning is the important postmodern idea that there are no over-arching 'myths' or stories which give a universal framework of meaning to language. The power of a grand narrative (or 'meta-narrative') uniting human beings across the world, into which local stories can integrate, has waned. It has been challenged as if it were a dictator restricting people's liberty. The thinker Jean-François Lyotard argues that a postmodern outlook demands a 'war on totality'[5] – a fight against any claim to universal meaning. This means that any world-view or framework of meaning is rubbished, whether that be the modern myth of progress, the Enlightenment myth of rational beings discovering truth or the Christian 'myth' that God made human beings and reveals himself to them. Of course, the only exception to this denial of over-arching stories is the over-arching idea that there are no over-arching ideas!

Language as power play

On top of the rejection of meta-narrative is the postmodern suspicion that any attempt to assign words particular objective meaning is to use force and assert power over others. The writer Michel Foucault argues that no firm foundations for knowledge exist at all, that there is no original or 'transcendental signified' (i.e. God) to which all 'signifiers' (human beings) can ultimately refer.[6] Clearly, this idea has direct consequences for the Christian seeking to advocate the possibility of encountering truth in Christ. But this is not all. Foucault goes on to argue that there is an essential interplay between knowledge and power. Echoing Nietzsche's phrase, 'the will to power', Foucault calls the pursuit of truth a 'will to knowledge' that arbitrarily establishes its own 'truth'. This 'truth' can then be imposed on others, giving power into the hands of the speaker or writer. In this way discourse and the pursuit of knowledge are written off as the pursuit of power, and this power is embodied and expressed in institutionalized languages:[7]

> Power produces knowledge ... There is no power relation
> without the correlative constitution of a field of knowledge,
> nor any knowledge that does not presuppose and constitute
> at the same time power relations ... [8]

This would mean that when we come to read the Bible, we must be suspicious of the writers, who are exercising power over us, and even more suspicious of anyone who might try to help us interpret the Bible. Any attempt at preaching from or explaining the Bible is purely a sinister attempt to gain power over another. This reminds me of a preacher in Oxford who got up into the pulpit one Sunday and preached his heart out. At the door of the church a young man shook his hand and began to look a little flushed. He had hated the sermon. When asked why this was, he replied that he had found it offensive that the preacher had talked with conviction – believing what he said to be true. He objected to the persuasive nature of what he had heard and was very suspicious of the power involved. This is the postmodern objection to meaning as power, expressed in a popular form. But again we see that the reasoning fails its own test. After all, one wonders how Foucault is able to tell us about power relations and words without falling into his own trap – how can he use words to explain this to us without himself taking power over us?

Presumably he is the one exceptional individual who can tell us things without taking power over us!

Truth

A further consequence of these ideas about power and manipulation is the denial of the idea of a disinterested knower, which means denying any possibility that we can stand beyond history and human society at a vantage point which could offer certain knowledge. Truth is not seen as theoretical or objective – rather, truth is a 'fabrication' or 'fiction', a 'system of ordered procedures for the production, regulation, distribution, circulation and operation of statements'.[9] Such a system of truth is seen as standing in a reciprocal relationship with systems of power that produce and sustain it. And so any attempt to assert truth about a historical event or any other kind of reality is perceived as power play. The suspicion is that a writer or speaker is trying to manipulate and control others. From this point of view the Bible is seen as a tool of manipulation – used by powerful people to control others.

The same question needs to be asked of this view – how can someone who believes this communicate it to others? If words are tools of oppression used by powerful people to control others, isn't Foucault doing exactly the same thing when he writes his philosophy books to tell us this? Once again, this argument falls at the first fence – it fails its own test. If the sceptical person wants to use this line of reasoning against the Bible, they need to be encouraged to see that it must also apply to their own reasoning. This reminds me very much of a friend's mother-in-law. She is constantly criticizing my friend and her husband for failing to telephone her regularly, but fairly frequently she goes travelling for a couple of months at a time without calling or letting her family know the details. Her complaint against her son is exactly what she herself does to her son. In human relationships this is called hypocrisy. In philosophical discussion this is called 'special pleading' – the rules apply to you but not to me. This kind of approach ought to be exposed for what it is.

Language and meaning

Further questions about language and meaning emerge when the knock-on effect of getting rid of God is felt. If God does not exist, there is no foundation for language and words are not able to signify or present any given reality. The thinker Jacques Derrida raises similar questions about words and language. He attacks what he calls 'logocentrism' and, more specifically, the view that our statements are representations of the world as it actually is apart from human activity. Derrida denies that language has any fixed meaning connected to a fixed reality and he denies that it unveils definitive truth. The belief that language can have meaning causes people to search for some ultimate word, presence, essence, truth or reality which can serve as the foundation of thought, language and experience – 'the transcendental signified'.[10] But he argues that such a God, or Idea, or World Spirit, does not actually exist. This interesting approach shows us that unless God exists, language cannot carry meaning. If we want to reject God, we have to undermine language.

If no such 'transcendental signified' exists, the meanings of words arise out of their relationship with an immediate context and not out of something more fixed and absolute. This would make language completely self-referential. Imagine how frustrating it would be if you had a sister or brother who insisted on interpreting your words to them as they pleased, with no reference to any fixed meaning for the given words. The simple request, 'Please do not borrow my clothes without my permission' could be easily interpreted to mean, 'Feel free to help yourself to my clothes at any time and leave them dirty and crumpled up on your bedroom floor.' If meaning changes over time and with changing contexts, the prospect of communication between one being and another is seriously jeopardized. Such a scenario would not only mean that texts are lost to us, but also the very capacity of humans to communicate with one another. Relationships would be completely undermined. And when it comes to reading, if the words within a text only have the meaning that I, in my cultural and linguistic context, give them, it would not be possible for that text to really speak to me. I would be speaking to myself. This is a serious objection and a real problem. However, this is only a problem if God does not exist and language has no capacity to carry real meaning. But if this were the case, we would not be able to assert it using words, because again the idea fails its own test.

We can see that a postmodern culture throws up all kinds of questions about the possibility of texts or words having any meaning. However, there is an interesting failure to recognize the inconsistency of thought here. After all, how can anyone tell us this? If words have no ultimate meaning, surely those who believe that should remain silent. Is it really possible to express this idea in words whilst at the same time denying those very words the

---

Postmodernism

- is the world-view which followed on the heels of modernism, coming to prominence in Western culture in the 1960s.
- is marked by disillusionment with and suspicion of the ideals of modernism such as certainty, idealistic trust in science and technology and an optimistic belief in the continual advancement of humanity.
- rejects any idea of a universal or absolute truth and therefore rejects the notion of one God over all.
- rejects any overarching story or meta-narrative by which one can make sense of the world.
- rejects any absolute morals.

possibility of meaning? If we are to escape complete silence, surely it is more credible to believe that some meaning is possible, that communication can occur.

The text of the Bible

If we are willing to concede that meaning might be possible, we need to begin to ask some questions about how we might read a text such as the Bible. One starting place could be the author. Probably the most important questions to ask about an author are to do with their intention in writing. When we come to look at the New Testament, and the Gospels in particular, two of the Gospel writers let us know what their intentions are. Luke wrote his Gospel as a Gentile believer in Jesus. He was a doctor, a scientific man. He had not had the privilege of being one of the twelve disciples who lived with Jesus for three years and knew him very well. He expresses his intentions in writing his Gospel at the beginning of his account:

> Many have undertaken to draw up an account of the things that have been fulfilled among us, just as they were handed down to us by those who from the first were eye-witnesses and servants of the word. Therefore, since I myself have carefully investigated everything from the beginning, it seemed good also to me to write an orderly account for you, most excellent Theophilus, so that you may know the certainty of the things you have been taught.
> (Luke 1:1–4)

John was one of the twelve disciples; he was very close to Jesus, having lived with him for three years and watched his ministry unfold. John is known as 'the beloved disciple', as it seems he was exceptionally close to Jesus. He expresses his intentions in writing his Gospel towards the end of it:

Jesus did many other miraculous signs in the presence of his disciples, which are not recorded in this book. But these are written that you may believe that Jesus is the Christ, the Son of God, and that by believing you may have life in his name. (John 20:30–31)

Now, I am not suggesting that because the authors give us their intentions, an unbeliever should automatically take these Gospels as 'gospel truth'. We can question and scrutinize the motives of the author and come up with a number of possibilities:

- It is possible that the author has genuine motives but has been deceived and is passing on mistaken information.
- It is possible that the author knows the information he is writing down is false and he is intentionally trying to deceive the reader.
- It is possible that the author has genuine motives and that, by and large, he is recording what actually happened.

We would then need to test these possibilities with specific reference to the text in question. There are two basic ways in which we could ask questions of the text – the inductive and the deductive. Inductive questions would ask whether the text of a Gospel makes sense of the world external to it. Could the reader make connections between what is in the text and the real world all around us? Or is this Gospel purely a circle of reality one has to step into, suspending the real world whilst within it? Do historical and archaeological references fit with the data available to us from the period? Does the text make sense of the world as we know it? Does it diagnose and adequately speak to the human condition? Does the text have the 'ring of truth'? All of these questions will help a seeker to think about whether a particular Gospel is trustworthy or even 'true'.

Deductive questions also need to be asked. It is interesting to me that many Christians try to start here without first addressing bigger-picture questions about the text. But although we do not begin here, these questions must still be asked. Does the text we are reading hold together? Is it internally coherent? Does it contradict itself? When we do step inside the text, does it make sense as a whole?

Testing for both deductive and inductive truth will help those outside the Christian faith to consider the Gospels and the rest of the New Testament for themselves. It is important for us as believers to resist the temptation to force others to accept what the Bible says 'because we say so'. Many people need to look at it first-hand, ask questions, scrutinize motives and encounter the reality of Jesus themselves in the pages of Scripture.

I remember meeting a sceptical non-Christian a number of years ago in Oxford. He had asked many questions about the Christian faith and had found some answers, but was still uncertain about exactly who Jesus was and whether we could trust the source materials about his life. As he read one of the Gospels he found himself questioning some of the miracles but was stunned to read that some of the original followers of Jesus were fishermen. When he read that fishermen saw the miracles and followed Jesus, he found himself strangely stirred. When I asked him why that was, he explained that he came from a family of fishermen in Scotland going back over many generations. He

---

Inductive questions ask whether the text of a Gospel makes sense of the world external to it. Could the reader make connections between what is in the text and the real world all around us? Or is this Gospel purely a circle of reality one has to step into, suspending the real world whilst within it?

Deductive questions ask whether the text of a Gospel makes sense in and of itself. Does the text we are reading hold together? Is it internally coherent? Does it contradict itself? When we do step inside the text, does it make sense as a whole?

knew that these were earthy people not given to hallucinations or being taken in by fraudulent miracles. He finished by saying, 'If those fishermen saw it, I believe they knew what they were talking about. I know people like that – they wouldn't be taken in easily. That is enough for me.' This is probably one of the stranger reasons I have been given for someone wanting to become a Christian. But as he tested the Gospels for truth, using his brain and his experience in life, he realized that the account he was reading did not just make sense internally as a document. It connected with reality for him personally.

Reader responsibility

Sometimes people ask me, 'You don't honestly believe the Bible literally, do you?' This has become an increasingly important question, as people are frightened of fundamentalism in the world around us. After September the 11th, they think that if people begin to believe what their holy books say, it is a very dangerous thing. To take a religious book literally is perceived as one of the most stupid and misguided things we can do. Of course, it is important to remember that it is not the act of believing what a book says or taking it literally that is necessarily dangerous. The danger is determined by the *content* of the book. What will we find when we read? Does the book incite violence; does it lend itself to a dangerous use? It cannot be an inherently evil thing to believe what a book says – the danger is dependent on the message.

So how do we answer the question, 'Should we take the Bible literally?' G. K. Chesterton was asked this question and wittily replied: 'The Bible says that Herod is a fox – that does not mean that he has a bushy tail and pointy ears. It also says that Jesus is the door – that does not mean that he is wooden, flat and swinging on hinges.' To assert that it is possible for a text to have meaning and to communicate that meaning to a reader or listener is not to take away entirely the responsibility of the reader or listener to participate in the process. The reader must ask questions about the author's intentions as well as scrutinizing their own motivations and reactions. The historical context of the text plays a part, as does the cultural context of the reader.

I would argue that to assert dogmatically that it is impossible for any text to have and communicate meaning is to be closed-minded. The Christian does not ask a sceptic to naively accept what the Bible says 'because we say so' but only to be open-minded enough to read a Gospel and ask questions of it, to scrutinize it and see for themselves whether or not what they find is compelling and truthful.

2 Can we know anything about history?

In our current cultural climate, which many call 'postmodernism', it has become unfashionable and, indeed, a little suspect to try to defend truth. This approach extends to historical truth, and our universities ring with the allegation that it is impossible for us to know for sure what happened in the past. History, we are told, is a matter of subjective opinion. The quest for historical truth should not be embarked upon at all – it is a fruitless, even impossible, exercise.

A few years ago I was involved in a university mission in Cambridge. I had been assigned to work in one of the colleges for the week and to try to address the different questions about Christianity that the students might have. On the first evening I was taken to the college bar to meet some people, and a guy came up to me to start a conversation. His opening line was: 'I hear that you are here to evangelize us. I think Christianity is a load of **** and I cannot believe that you are here to try and tell us about it.' Not knowing what else to do, I simply stammered, 'That's interesting. Why do you say that?' He went on: 'I have been in a choir since I was eight years old. That means I have been to church every day of my life for eleven years. I know there is nothing in it.' And, probably because I didn't respond very quickly, he added scornfully, 'Why are *you* a Christian?' This is a brilliant question, to which I was able to reply: 'There are lots of reasons why I am a Christian, but let me just give you two. Christianity is intellectually robust and opens itself to our scrutiny, and it is existentially satisfying.' In other words, it makes sense and it is real in my experience. He looked a bit surprised and said: 'I've heard people talk about their experiences of God and I don't buy that one – but what do you mean about it being intellectually robust?' We went on to talk about some of the reasons for belief in God and some of the evidence around the person of Christ. It was during that conversation that I found this question of history being raised very powerfully. As the compelling evidence for the historicity of Christ, his cross and his resurrection was laid out, the best defence available to my new friend was to deny the possibility of knowing any history at all. As I explained some of the ideas we are going to look at in this chapter, it became clear that this person had never been seriously challenged about the person of Christ before. He ended our conversation by saying, 'I have been to church almost every day of my life. Why has no-one told me any of this before?'

The loss of certainty

We need to understand the cultural context of this broad-brush-stroke denial of the possibility of knowing what happened in history. The rejection of certainty with regard to history is part of a larger movement in our society characterized by disillusion-ment with any kind of certainty. This is expressed in a number of ways in our culture, whether that be a growing frustration with the ideal of scientific progress or an increasing distrust of the statements made by various authorities, whether they be political, judicial or educational. Truth is not as simple as we once thought – as a society we are now sceptical of any form of certainty.

In this context of a generation that is confused and hurting, a person with any kind of certainty or conviction is an anomaly. David Bowie, interviewed in the *Sunday Times* magazine, put it like this:

> John Lennon, Pete Townsend and I all had this same thing of rather cobbling together one's own belief system – in my case, one that changes all the time as I need to change it. Because I cannot really come to grips with absolutism. I'm fascinated by characters like Sir Thomas More. I think it's because it is so alien to how I seem to cope with life. I can't understand how people can be like that. They are exotic creatures to me. How do they get to that place where they know with absolute certainty what's true?[1]

As we shall see in this chapter, this ambivalence in one's approach to truth extends into the territory of history. It cannot only be in matters of religion that there is no such thing as truth. History too is up for grabs. We cannot be certain about what happened in the past – all views are equally valid, and so definite historical truth is ultimately unknowable.

It is hardly surprising, then, that many people are incredulous that Christians (even those who seem to be quite intelligent) believe that the Bible records historical truth about the person of Christ and many other things. How can we be so sure? Surely all historical literature, including biblical histories like the Gospels, must be inherently suspicious. But if we cannot know anything in history, even recent history is up for grabs. The theologian E. P. Sanders goes so far as to say that 'historical events could not be verified even if we had a video recording.'[2] And so follows the question: 'How can you expect me to follow this Jesus of yours if I can't be certain about the texts that give me access to him?' The idea that history is beyond our grasp is incredibly powerful. And yet, when we begin to look at the consequences of this idea and the reasoning upon which it is based, that which seemed a compelling edifice begins to crumble.

How do we have access to history?

In the mid nineteenth century most Western historians conceived of history as an exact science. Facts could be presented objectively, giving the reader direct and accurate access to the events of the past. The historian Leopold von Ranke typified this approach, stating that the historian must present the past as it actually happened. By the 1920s the ideal of pure historical objectivity began to come under fire. It was James Harvey Robinson who joked that objective history is just history without an object. Suddenly history could only be a matter of interpretation. Personal interpretations of various texts had become the vogue among historians. Historical relativism received a new lease of life in the 1960s in collaboration with deconstructionist philosophers and became a central tenet of the intellectual trend often called 'postmodernism'. The postmodernist historiographer Greg Dening argues that recorded history is no more than an illusion of the past and that in reality it is determined by the cultural context and personal preferences of the historian. He claims, 'History is something we make rather than something we learn.' He goes so far as to say: 'I want to persuade them that any history they make will be fiction.'[3] The content of any historical document will be entirely biased by the author's ambition and the cultural context of the text, amongst other things. Therefore the idea that the text is capable of conveying a true representation of what actually happened is rejected.

Foucault goes slightly further than this, arguing that history can make no claim to be entirely free of values or neutral, and therefore he concludes that, as the desire to know the past cannot come from a disinterested quest for truth, it must arise from a desire to control the past for some purpose or other.[4] His conception of the will to power through knowledge emerges again, but now with regard not to literature but to historical narratives.

In our discussion of the Bible – and, more specifically for the seeker, the New Testament Gospels – as history, we need to grasp that this nervousness about history has wide-reaching implications. Not only is history unknowable, but those who seek to bring history to bear on the present have some motivation of power and control in doing so. They are imposing their perspectives and ideas on others in a classic form of Foucault's 'will to power'. Any Christian seeking to make Christ's life, death and resurrection known to others can therefore be written off in this way.

But the question remains – should history really be viewed in such terms, and can a sceptic really be consistent and honest in taking this approach not only with the Bible but with other more recent historical events? A historical event which, in my experience, helps bring this question into sharp focus for us is the Holocaust. In fact the serious consequences of this idea that we cannot know what has happened in history are sharply underlined for us by the fact that it has opened the door to the Holocaust denial movement. It is, of course, ironic that with any mention of Holocaust denial, a discussion of historical relativism is usually dropped. But the truth is that within this highly publicized genre, revisionist scholars are even calling recent history into question. Because of the compulsory ambiguity and uncertainty about truth that so many academics now insist on, events just fifty short years in the past can be legitimately denied. And, as if this were not enough, the view that the Holocaust did not happen must be given as much credence as the view that it did happen!

This is where historical relativism falls down. It simply implodes. It must be possible for us to know with some certainty what happened in the past. All views of history are not equally valid – we need to be able to draw some distinctions between history and pseudo-history. There are some standards of verification, ways of matching up fact and interpretation, which are plausible and recognizable by most of us.

We may reject the pure historical objectivity of the nineteenth century. But surely a realistic and balanced approach leads us to a *via media* between illogical, nihilistic relativism and the steely optimism of pure objectivity. This pragmatic approach, which recognizes both the possibility of access to history and the frailty of many historical sources, is championed by the historian James Kloppenberg, who calls his approach 'pragmatic hermeneutics':

> Beyond the noble dream of scientific objectivity and the nightmare of complete relativism lies the terrain of pragmatic truth, which provides us with hypotheses, provisional syntheses, imaginative but warranted interpretations which then provide the basis for continuing inquiry and experimentation ... Historical truth – like all truth in a world that has moved beyond the discredited dualisms of both positivism and idealism – must be made, questioned and reinterpreted. As historians we cannot aspire to more than a pragmatic hermeneutics that relies on the methods of science and the interpretation of meanings. But we should not aspire to less.[5]

Converging lines of evidence

The method is simply this: we have access to historical truth via converging lines of evidence. So, then, the Holocaust, like other historical events, is accessible to us through several different kinds of evidence which add together to give us a reliable picture of what happened. We have written documents including thousands of letters, memos, bills, orders, speeches, articles and confessions. We have eyewitness testimony both from Jewish survivors and SS perpetrators, from local townspeople and high-ranking Nazis. Then there are the photographs, including military, press, civilian and aerial images taken by both German and Allied photographers. There are also the remains of the camps themselves existing in varying degrees of originality. And finally there is the inferential evidence – the population demographics from the pre-World War 2 era which show that approximately 6 million European Jews disappeared. There must be an explanation for all of this – the evidence points to the historicity of the Holocaust.

The American general, Dwight D. Eisenhower, was called upon to inspect the Nazi death camps immediately after the war, and he spoke of 'indisputable evidence of Nazi brutality'. He wrote after the events, recording history – admittedly recent history, and it comes to us just sixty years after what had taken place. Eisenhower's diary records his reaction to what he observed:

> I visited every nook and cranny of the camp because I felt it my duty to be in a position from then on to testify at first hand about these things in case there ever grew up at home the belief or assumption that 'the stories of Nazi brutality were just propaganda.' Some members of the visiting party were unable to go through the ordeal. I not only did so but as soon as I returned to Patten's headquarters that evening I sent communications to both Washington and London, urging the 2 governments to send instantly to Germany a random group of newspaper editors and representative groups from the national legislatures. I felt that the evidence should be immediately placed before the American and British publics in a fashion that would leave no room for cynical doubt.[6]

With foreboding insight Eisenhower predicted the possibility of future generations attempting to deny that such horrific events had taken place.

It is true that with a purely relativist approach to history, and without the use of the convergent historical evidences, we are forced to become agnostic concerning the events of even the twentieth century. Those who argue for the impossibility of historical truth with regard to the Bible also deny more recent history with their same arguments. If history is purely relative, a matter of personal opinion, it is not only the Bible that is challenged. Every event which has taken place in history must be suspect, whether it be Stalin's purges, Hitler's Holocaust or the arrival of William the Conqueror in 1066. We deny the possibility of knowing history through converging lines of evidence at great cost.

The relativizing of all history extends beyond the events of World War 2 to the historical person of Christ as he is presented in the Gospel accounts and other historical documents. And yet such an approach rings hollow when we begin to scratch beneath the surface. Just as Eisenhower recorded what he had seen and compiled information from various sources in order to present to others what had really happened, so the writer of Luke's Gospel compiles his report from eyewitnesses and other evidence so that Gentiles like himself, who had not seen Jesus in action in first-century Palestine, could have access to what happened. The overlap of intention between Luke and Eisenhower is quite striking. Luke begins his Gospel with the words:

> Therefore, since I myself have carefully investigated every-thing from the beginning, it seemed good also to me to write an orderly account for you, most excellent Theophilus, so that you may know the certainty of the things you have been taught.
> (Luke 1:3–4)

Luke and the other Gospel writers recorded the events that had taken place with scrupulous accuracy. Their intention in writing was that we as future generations could read about Christ confidently, knowing that historians had thoroughly researched and compiled the material in a rigorous way.

If we cannot defend the possibility of access to history, whether that be events that happened 60 years ago or 2,000 years ago, the consequences are huge. Many sensitive, intelligent people do not wish to go down this route. There may follow a reluctance to accept the historicity of the content of the New Testament, but that is a very different matter from a blanket denial of the possibility of knowing any history at all.

3 Are the biblical manuscripts reliable?

Following on from questions about interpretation and history, at some point it may become necessary to think about the manuscript tradition which underlies the Bible. The Bible tops the bestseller lists every year and world sales of the Bible are well over 100 million every year. One journalist writes:

> Forget modern British novelists and TV tie-ins, the Bible is the best-selling book every year. If sales of the Bible were included in best-seller lists, it would be a rare week when anything else would achieve a look in. It is wonderful, weird . . . that in this godless age . . . this one book should go on selling, every month.[1]

The Bible is not just one book; it is a collection of 66 books which are divided into two sections. There are 39 books in the first, largest part, the Old Testament, and 27 in the New Testament. The Bible was written over a period of 1,600 years by more than 40 authors. These people came from all kinds of different backgrounds – kings, diplomats, poor people, fishermen, tentmakers.

The Bible was originally written in three languages – Hebrew, Aramaic and Greek, and it was written on three continents – Asia, Africa and Europe. The vast spread of the Bible's social, geographical and cultural original contexts is then followed by a multiplication of these diversities as the manuscripts were copied and spread throughout the known world. This means that there are a vast number of ancient manuscripts to be examined and the text of the Bible is extremely well attested.

The integrity of any ancient writing is determined by the number of documented manuscripts or fragments of manuscripts which still exist. For example, there are less than ten existing copies of the ancient manuscripts of Plato. These can be studied and compared in order to determine the accuracy and quality of the transmission of his writings throughout the years. The oldest of these manuscripts is a copy dating about 1,400 years after the work in question was originally written. This text is respected and read in the present day. When it comes to the Bible, there are over 5,000 handwritten manuscripts in the Greek language in support of the New Testament alone that help us ensure the accuracy of its writings. Many of the earliest copies are separated from the originals not by 1,400 years, but by only 25 to 50 years.

Manuscript matters

During the early Christian era, the writing material most commonly used was *papyrus*. This is a highly durable reed from the Nile Valley. It was glued together much like plywood is today, and then laid out to dry in the sun. In the twentieth century many remnants of documents (both biblical and non-biblical) on papyrus have been discovered, especially in the dry, arid lands of North Africa and the Middle East.

Another material used was *parchment*. This was made from the skin of sheep or goats, and was in widespread use until the late Middle Ages, when paper began to replace it. It was scarce and expensive; hence, it was used almost exclusively for documents which were considered to be especially important.

There are more than 5,300 known Greek manuscripts of the New Testament. Add 10,000 Latin manuscripts and 9,300 early portions of the New Testament, and we have around 24,000 extant manuscript copies of portions of the New Testament. No other document from antiquity approaches this. The nearest is Homer's *Iliad* with 634 manuscripts. The first complete text of Homer dates from the thirteenth century AD, although there are much earlier fragments of manuscripts. The scholar John Warwick Montgomery comments:

> to be sceptical of the resultant text of the New Testament books is to allow all of classical antiquity to slip into obscurity, for no documents of the ancient period are as well attested bibliographically as the New Testament.[2]

Manuscript evidence for ancient writings				
Author	Written	Earliest fragment/copy	Time span	Number of MSS.
Caesar	100–44 BC	AD 900	1,000 yrs	10
Plato	427–347 BC	AD 900	1,200 yrs	7
Thucydides	460–400 BC	AD 900	1,300 yrs	8
Tacitus	AD 100	AD 1100	1,000 yrs	20
Suetonius	AD 75–160	AD 950	800 yrs	8
Homer (*Iliad*)	900 BC	400 BC	500 yrs	643
New Testament	AD 40–100	AD 125	25–50 yrs	24,000

F. F. Bruce comments:

> There is no body of ancient literature in the world which enjoys such a wealth of good textual attestation as the New Testament.

In fact in his book, *The Bible and Archaeology*, Sir Frederic G. Kenyon, former director and principal librarian of the British Museum, stated about the New Testament:

> The interval, then, between the dates of original composition and the earliest extant evidence becomes so small as to be in fact negligible, and the last foundation for any doubt that the Scriptures have come down to us substantially as they were written has now been removed. Both the authenticity and the general integrity of the books of the New Testament may be regarded as finally established.[3]

Good examples of ancient New Testament manuscripts are the Codex Vaticanus and the Codex Siniaticus, which are parchment copies of the entire New Testament dating from the fourth century (AD 325–450). Earlier still, there are fragments and papyrus copies of portions of the New Testament dating from 100 to 200 years (AD 180–225) before Vaticanus and Siniaticus. The especially clear ones are the Chester Beatty Papyrus (P45, P46, P47) and the Bodmer Papyrus II, XIV, XV (P46, P75). From these five manuscripts alone, we can construct all of Luke, John, Romans, 1 and 2 Corinthians, Galatians, Ephesians, Philippians, Colossians, 1 and 2 Thessalonians, Hebrews, and portions of Matthew, Mark, Acts and Revelation. Only the Pastoral Epistles (Titus, 1 and 2 Timothy), the General Epistles (James, 1 and 2 Peter, and 1, 2 and 3 John) and Philemon are excluded.

One of the very oldest portions of the Bible surviving today is a fragment of a papyrus codex containing John 18:31–33, 37. It is called the Rylands Papyrus (P52) and dates from AD 130. It was found in Egypt and has caused academics to place the Fourth Gospel back into the first century, abandoning a nineteenth-century assertion that it could not have been written then by the Apostle John.

Quotations from the New Testament in the writings of the church Fathers also seem to point to the relatively early completion of the New Testament. German scholarship of the nineteenth and early twentieth centuries argued for the New Testament having been written a couple of hundred years after the events it recorded. This led to many people distrusting the content of the New Testament, believing that it was made up by the church a long time after the events in order to rewrite history. However, as well as the discovery of early fragments of the New Testament, the writings of the church Fathers provide us with good evidence for a short period of time between the events themselves and the Gospels which describe them. For example, the Epistle of Clement to the Corinthians (dated AD 95) cites verses from the Gospels, Acts, Romans, 1 Corinthians, Ephesians, Titus, Hebrews, and 1 Peter. The letters of Ignatius (dated AD 115) were written to several churches in Asia Minor and cite verses from Matthew, John, Romans, 1 and 2 Corinthians, Galatians, Ephesians, Philippians, 1 and 2 Timothy and Titus. These letters indicate that the entire New Testament was written within the first century AD. There is, of course, other internal evidence for a first-century date for the writing of the New Testament. The book of Acts ends abruptly with Paul in prison, awaiting trial (28:30–31). It is likely that Luke wrote Acts during this time, before Paul finally appeared before Caesar. This would be about AD 62–3, meaning that Acts and Luke's Gospel were written within thirty years of the ministry and death of Jesus. Further evidence of this is that there is no mention of the destruction of Jerusalem in AD 70. Although Matthew, Mark and Luke record Jesus' prophecy that the temple and city would be destroyed within that generation (Matthew 24:1–2; Mark 13:1–2; Luke 21:5–9, 20–24, 32), no New Testament book refers to this event as having happened. It is likely that letters written after AD 70 would have mentioned this fulfilment of Jesus' prophecy.

In addition to the actual Greek manuscripts, there are more than 1,000 copies and fragments of the New Testament in Syrian, Coptic, Armenian, Gothic and Ethiopic, as well as 8,000 copies of the Latin Vulgate, some of which date back almost to Jerome's original translation in AD 384–400. As has already been mentioned, a further witness to the New Testament text is found in the thousands of quotations which are dispersed throughout the writings of the church Fathers. In fact there are 86,000 quotations – this means that if all the ancient New Testament manuscripts were somehow to disappear overnight, it would still be possible to reconstruct the entire New Testament with quotations from the church Fathers, with the exception of about twenty verses!

The Dead Sea Scrolls

The Dead Sea Scrolls are made up of 40,000 inscribed fragments, and from these fragments more than 500 books have been reconstructed. The writings are biblical as well as commentaries on the Old Testament and writings on the Qumran community itself. Ralph Earle gives an account of the discovery of the scrolls:

> The story of this discovery is one of the most fascinating tales of modern times. In February or March of 1947 a Bedouin shepherd boy named Muhammad was searching for a lost goat. He tossed a stone into a hole in a cliff on the west side of the Dead Sea about 8 miles south of Jericho. To his surprise he heard the sound of shattering pottery. Investigating, he discovered an amazing sight. On the floor of the cave were several large jars containing leather scrolls wrapped in linen cloth. Because the jars were carefully sealed, the scrolls had been preserved in excellent condition for nearly 1,900 years.

They had been placed there in AD 68.

The scrolls and the Old Testament

The Dead Sea Scrolls include a complete copy of the book of Isaiah, a fragmented copy of Isaiah containing much of chapters

38 – 60, and fragments of almost every book in the Old Testament. The majority of the fragments are from Isaiah and the Pentateuch (Genesis, Exodus, Leviticus, Numbers and Deuteronomy). The books of Samuel, in a tattered copy, were also found, as well as two complete chapters of the book of Habakkuk. In addition, there were found a number of non-biblical scrolls related to the Qumran commune.

These materials are dated around 100 BC. The significance of the find, and particularly the copy of Isaiah, was recognized by Merrill F. Unger when he said:

> This complete document of Isaiah quite understandably
> created a sensation since it was the first major Biblical
> manuscript of great antiquity ever to be recovered.
> Interest in it was especially keen since it antedates by
> more than a thousand years the oldest Hebrew texts
> preserved in the Masoretic tradition.[4]

Before the discovery of the scrolls, the oldest known manuscript was written 1,300 years after the writing of the complete Old Testament. After the finding of the scrolls, the problem was then to ascertain how accurate these manuscripts were in relation to what was originally written. Because the text had been copied many times, could it be trusted? One of the scrolls had a complete copy of Isaiah in Hebrew. It is dated by paleographers around 125 BC; with the Masoretic text being dated AD 916, this makes a difference of 1,000 years. If, upon examination, there were little or no textual changes in those Masoretic texts where comparisons were possible, an assumption could then be made that the Masoretic Scribes had probably been just as faithful in their copying of the other biblical texts which could not be compared with the Qumran material.

The accuracy is astonishing for an ancient manuscript and is word for word identical with our standard Hebrew Bible in 95% of the text. In the other 5% there are only minor variations. To give an example:

Of the 166 words in Isaiah 53 there are 17 letters in question: 10 of these are a matter of spelling which does not affect the sense; 4 are minor stylistic changes, such as conjunctions. The remaining 3 letters comprise the word 'light' which is added in verse 11 and does not affect the meaning greatly. In fact the use of 'light' here is supported by two other manuscripts, the LXX ('the Septuagint', the Greek translation of the Old Testament) and the 1Q Isa ('Isaiah A', a copy of Isaiah found in Cave 1 at Qumran).

Millar Burrows concludes:

> It is a matter of wonder that through something like a thousand years the text underwent so little alteration. As I said in my first article on the scroll, 'Herein lies its chief importance, supporting the fidelity of the Masoretic tradition.'[5]

Biblical passage	Cave/Fragment	Date
Mark 4:28	7Q6	AD 50
Mark 6:48	7Q15	AD?
Mark 6:52–53	7Q5	AD 50
Mark 12:17	7Q7	AD 50
Acts 27:38	7Q6	AD 60
Romans 5:11–12	7Q9	AD 70+
1 Timothy 3:16; 4:1–3	7Q4	AD 70+
2 Peter 1:15	7Q10	AD 70+
James 1:23–24	7Q8	AD 70+

The scrolls and the New Testament

Some of the Dead Sea Scroll fragments seem to be pieces of the New Testament. Considering the fact that Qumran was closed and sealed before the fall of Jerusalem in AD 70, this is a startling possibility.

Fragments found by the Jesuit palaeographer José O'Callahan in 1972 in Cave 7, which had previously been categorized as 'not identified' and listed under 'biblical texts', are controversially believed by some to contain New Testament passages. The table on page 44 shows us what was found in Qumran Cave 7.

Critics have argued that these are not fragments of New Testament manuscripts but are instead writings produced by the Qumran community which sound similar to New Testament passages. The fact that the fragments are so small makes it extremely difficult to be certain either way. However, if, as seems highly possible, these fragments are pieces of the New Testament, these discoveries are potentially hugely significant.

Although many of us are not experts on ancient texts and fragments and may find ourselves glazing over as we think about all these facts and figures, it is important that we realize that statements which are frequently trotted out, such as, 'The Bible has been changed', should not go unchallenged. The sceptic who is looking at the Bible and asking questions about it will find that its manuscript traditions are open to scrutiny and can stand up under it.

4 Is the content of the manuscripts reliable?

It may well come as a shock to some that the manuscript tradition of the Old and New Testaments stands up to rigorous scrutiny. There is a widespread belief that much of the Bible was written centuries after the events it records and that it has been changed and tampered with on the whim of different scribes or interested parties. The breadth and age of the existing ancient manuscripts tell a very different story. However, the next question is invariably: 'Just because the manuscripts are reliable, that doesn't make the content of them true.' Indeed, it is true that no-one argues for the historicity of Homer's mythology. The manuscripts of his writings may be reasonably intact, but that does not make what he was writing about reliable or accurate historical material. Aren't the Gospels on the same kind of level – aren't they just mythological, with true moral value but very little historical reality? Surely accounts involving people walking on water and water turning into wine weren't meant to be taken as historically true – it's all mythology, isn't it?'

These questions are all very important, and it is true that the Christian must not assume that an unbeliever will accept the content of the biblical text as true, simply because the manuscripts themselves have proved to be so trustworthy. There are a number of questions tied up here. The first issue is to do with our approach to the supernatural world. It is probably true to say that our postmodern society is much more open to the possibility of a supernatural realm than was the Enlightenment modernist world-view of previous generations. However, scepticism about these things does still exist in some portions of the population, and it is important for us to deal with the underlying reasons for this.

Scepticism about the supernatural world

One possible reason for disbelieving the content of the Gospels and the rest of the Bible is its recording of powerful miraculous events. What is the cause of this disbelief? Is the person assuming a framework in which miracles are a logical impossibility? Has this individual closed their mind to the possibility of miracles and supernatural occurrences? Do they believe only in the natural world and things which are scientifically provable? This scepticism is based on the ideas of the philosopher David Hume (1711–76). He argued that all objects of human inquiry are either 'relations of ideas' (i.e. mathematical statements and definitions) or 'matters of fact' (i.e. everything which can be known and tested empirically). Hume wrote:

> When we run over libraries, persuaded of these principles,
> what havoc must we make? If we take in our hand any
> volume – of divinity or school metaphysics, for instance –
> let us ask, does it contain any abstract reasoning concerning
> quantity or number? No. Does it contain any experimental
> reasoning concerning matter of fact and existence? No.
> Commit it then to the flames, for it can contain nothing
> but sophistry and illusion.[1]

However, there are serious problems with this position. The main one is that Hume's philosophy fails its own test, because his own statement fits into neither of his categories. As Norman Geisler comments:

the statement that 'only analytic or empirical propositions are meaningful' is not itself an analytic (true by definition) or empirical statement. Hence, by its own criteria it is meaningless.[2]

C. S. Lewis deals with this kind of materialist approach in his usual lucid manner, showing that a dogmatic commitment to this philosophy makes thinking itself problematic:

It follows that no account of the universe can be true unless that account leaves it possible for our thinking to be a real insight. A theory which explained everything else in the whole universe but which made it impossible to believe that our thinking was valid would be utterly out of court. For that theory would itself have been reached by thinking ... Thus a strict materialism refutes itself for the reasons given long ago by Professor Haldane: 'If my mental processes are determined wholly by the motions of atoms in my brain, I have no reason to suppose that my beliefs are true ... and hence I have no reason for supposing my brain to be composed of atoms.'[3]

This kind of passionate commitment to a purely material world and the non-possibility of miraculous interventions from outside is problematic. For the materialist, thinking itself becomes a process which falls outside of the remit of that which has capacity for meaning.

The motivation for denying the possible existence of a supernatural realm often seems to be strong, even to the point of demonstrating prejudice. One writer who comes from a materialist viewpoint considers this phenomenon:

It is not that the methods and institutions of science somehow compel us to accept a material explanation of the phenomenal world but on the contrary, that we are forced by our *a priori* adherence to material causes to create an apparatus of investigation and a set of concepts that produce material explanations, no matter how counter-intuitive, no matter how mystifying to the uninitiated. Moreover, that materialism is an absolute, for we cannot allow a divine foot in the door.[4]

A commitment to the modernist world-view, in which there is nothing other than the empirically testable world around us, means that everything else is seen through a materialist lens (although this lens, of course, is not acknowledged and does not even pass its own test). This kind of *a priori* commitment to the falseness of the Gospels and the non-possibility of any miraculous occurrence is a form of closed-mindedness. The basis on which these views are held – that is, philosophical materialism – is not itself logically consistent and deserves to be challenged. Materialists need to be encouraged to at least be open to the possibility of the supernatural, even if they remain extremely sceptical. To be closed to this possibility is to claim absolute knowledge of the universe – an astounding 'god-like' claim.

New Testament miracles

It may be interesting for a sceptic to look at the context of the New Testament miracles. Many of the men and women involved were fishermen or tax collectors, certainly 'down-to-earth' types. We read that when Jesus walked on water they were frightened. This is an ordinary reaction to a supernatural event; it is a response that rings true. The reader is being told about these events with the acknowledgment that they are unusual. We are expected to be surprised that these things happened. We read that when Joseph discovered that Mary was pregnant, he wanted to put her away. Again, this is a normal human reaction – he assumes a natural reason for the pregnancy, and is only convinced otherwise by a supernatural experience himself. For a person who is sceptical about the possibility of the miraculous, it may be important to read a Gospel themselves. Many people who have this outlook have never really picked up a Gospel and read it. They may expect it to be a story full of goblins and fairies, not the down-to-earth but marvellous writing that it is.

Intentional deception?

Just because the manuscript tradition is well attested does not mean that the content contained within it is truthful. While the manuscripts may be genuine ancient copies leaving no room for a hoax, this does not mean that what is written in them is not an attempt at deception. This question may be phrased along the following lines: 'The stories were all invented by the writers as a deliberate attempt to inspire followers and to exonerate the disciples' decision to follow this man Jesus. He didn't ever want to found a religion but his followers did.' There are a number of ways of answering this question:

1. Why would the disciples portray themselves in a bad light (e.g. Peter's denial; their slowness to understand Jesus' teaching; their lack of faith)?
2. Why is there so much in the New Testament about the cost of Christianity? Surely they would have given it up after all the suffering, if it was a deception.
3. Why would they be willing to be killed for their teachings? For example, Peter was crucified upside down, and Thomas was torn in half.
4. As John Stott says: 'If anything is clear from the Gospels and the Acts it is that the apostles were sincere. They may have been deceived, if you like, but they were not deceivers. Hypocrites and martyrs are not made of the same stuff.'

Is the New Testament comprehensible?

We should remember that many people today have the idea that the Bible is gobbledegook. However, a comparison between the Scriptures and rival literature shows the coherence of the Gospels. Let us take a section of the apocryphal *Gospel of Thomas* as an example:

Jesus said, 'I have cast fire on the world and behold, I guard it until it blazes.' Jesus said, 'This heaven will pass away and that which is above it will pass away, and the dead were not alive and the living will not die. In the days when you ate what is dead you made it alive; when you come into the light what will you do? On the day when you were one you became two. But when you have become two what will you do?'[5]

The straightforward style of the New Testament Gospels is in stark contrast to this rambling alternative. Even Jesus' more apocalyptic statements contained in the New Testament Gospels have a coherence and comprehensible style which is notably lacking here.

Other ancient literature

Sceptics would be surprised by the number of extra-biblical writings which refer to events and places mentioned by the writers of the Bible. These writings come from a variety of perspectives and backgrounds, demonstrating that at least some of the content of the Bible is credible to the sceptic.

Josephus

Josephus was born in AD 37 into a Jewish family, and he joined the Pharisaic party at the age of nineteen. He settled in Rome where he lived under the name of 'Flavius Josephus'. He wrote prolifically, and it is in the pages of his books *History of the Jewish War* and *Antiquities of the Jewish People* that we come across various references to biblical characters, places and events. He mentions:

1. *Figures from the New Testament*. The Herods, Pilate, Felix, Festus, the procurators of Judea, the high priestly families of Annas, Caiaphas and Ananias – all these people are referred to by Josephus. He also mentions Judas the Galilean who led an uprising (see Acts 5:37), and at another point 'James the brother of the so-called Christ'.

2. *Events mentioned by the New Testament*. The famine in the days of Claudius (see Acts 11:28).

3. *The crucifixion of Jesus*. Josephus writes:

> And there arose about this time Jesus, a wise man, if indeed we should call him a man; for he was a doer of marvellous deeds, a teacher of men who receive the truth with pleasure. He led away many Jews, and also many of the Greeks. This man was the Christ. And when Pilate had condemned him to the cross on his impeachment by the chief men among us, those who had loved him at first did not cease; for he appeared to them on the third day alive again, the divine prophets having spoken these and thousands of other wonderful things about him; and even now the tribe of Christians, so named after him, has not yet died out.[6]

This passage is controversial and should be handled with care, as many scholars have argued that it is a later interpolation by Christians, trying to prove something about Jesus. It is dismissed on the grounds that Josephus, a Jew, would not have written so positively about the Christian claims about Jesus. However, I have included it here as a useful reference, because other scholars argue that the earliest copies of Jospehus contain this paragraph, and so if this is an interpolation, a lot more of his writing must be held in question. These scholars also argue that Josephus is speaking in jest and is mocking those who believe in Jesus, and that the overall tone of the passage is heavy with irony and scorn. If this is the case, it is a useful historical document which mentions the bare facts of Christian belief about Jesus the historical person, and as such deserves our attention.

Thallus

Thallus wrote a work tracing the history of Greece and its relations with Asia from the time of the Trojan War to his own day (AD 52). None of his own manuscripts survive, but he is referred to by Julius Africanus in AD 221. This is interesting, because Thallus had written about the darkness over the land following Christ's crucifixion and had tried to dismiss the darkness as being of no religious importance. But by trying to dismiss it, he gives us a historical reference to it. Julius Africanus writes: 'Thallus, in the third book of his histories, explains away this darkness as an eclipse of the sun – unreasonably, it seems to me' – unreasonably, because it was Passover and hence the time of the full moon.[7]

Tacitus

Tacitus wrote a history of Rome around AD 110. When recording the time of Nero, he wrote about that emperor's horrific decision to burn Rome down:

> Therefore to scotch the rumour, Nero substituted as culprits and punished with the utmost refinements of cruelty, a class of men loathed for their vices whom the crowd styled Christians. Christus, from whom they got their name, had been executed by sentence of the procurator Pontius Pilate when Tiberius was emperor; and the pernicious superstition was checked for a short time, only to break out afresh, not only in Judea, the home of the plague, but in Rome itself, where all the horrible and shameful things in the world collect and find a home.[8]

Here we have brief but credible references to the basic facts concerning the death of Christ under Pontius Pilate.

Suetonius

Suetonius wrote biographies of the first twelve Caesars. In his *Life of Nero* he writes: 'Punishment was inflicted on the Christians, a class of men addicted to a novel and mischievous superstition.'[9] In his *Life of Claudius* he says: 'As the Jews were making constant disturbances at the instigation of Chrestus, he expelled them from Rome.'[10]

Plinius Secundus (Pliny the Younger)

Pliny was governor of Bithynia in Asia Minor from AD 111 to AD 113, and he wrote a number of letters to the Emperor Trajan during these two years. In one of these letters he asked for advice on how to deal with Christians:

> they were in the habit of meeting on a certain fixed day before it was light, when they sang an anthem to Christ as God, and bound themselves by a solemn oath not to commit any wicked deed, but to abstain from all fraud, theft and adultery, never to break their word, or deny a trust when called upon to honour it; after which it was their custom to separate, and then meet again to partake of food, but food of an ordinary kind.[11]

Has the Bible been changed in transmission?

So we have seen a few examples of extra-biblical historical writers making reference to biblical events, and lending credence to the accuracy of those events. Another question which often follows on from this one (i.e. about the reliability of the content of the biblical record) concerns whether the Bible has been tampered with by different copyists. Some people have an image in their minds of many generations of scribes reproducing the biblical manuscripts for distribution, and each generation adding its own changes, so that what we have now bears little resemblance to the original and cannot be trusted.

However, the reality is that the textual variants that do exist are mostly single letters or grammatical differences. Our modern translations are extremely forthcoming at mentioning these minor differences; they are not hidden away but clearly noted and referenced in the margins and footnotes on each page. When we bear in mind that we are talking about large numbers of ancient, hand-copied manuscripts (around 24,000 manuscript copies for the New Testament alone), the Bible we have today is astoundingly free from questions. The scholar Norman Geisler comments:

> Only about one-eighth of all the variants had any weight as most of them are merely mechanical matters such as spelling or style. Of the whole, then, only about one-sixtieth rise above 'trivialities' or can in any sense be called 'substantial variations'.[12]

The Talmudists

The Old Testament text is similarly robust. The Talmudists reproduced Old Testament manuscripts between AD 270 and AD 500. They were religious scholars who commented on and explained the Old Testament to the Jewish community. They had an intricate set of regulations which they followed in order to ensure the integrity of the manuscripts they were producing.[13]

The Masoretes

The Masoretes took on the laborious job of editing and standardizing the Old Testament text between AD 500 and AD 900, working from the manuscripts that were available to them. F. F. Bruce writes:

> with the greatest imaginable reverence, they devised a complicated system of safeguard against scribal slips. They

counted, for example, the number of times each letter of the alphabet occurs in each book; they pointed out the middle letter of the Pentateuch and the middle letter of the whole Hebrew Bible, and made even more detailed calculations than these.[14]

This kind of respect for the integrity of the text is important for us to remember, if we are to gain a true picture of how the Bible has been transmitted from ancient times until today. Popular images of ancient scribes making things up as they went along, and changing texts at will, are a travesty of what actually happened. The motivation of those who transmitted the texts was that successive generations would be able to find truth for themselves in the pages of Scripture. The integrity of the content of Scripture was of paramount importance to them. We now have to make our own minds up about whether that content is actually true or not, but to hide behind an idea that it has been corrupted and changed in transmission is a little disingenuous.

5 What about the canon?

As we consider what to make of the Bible and ask questions about its trustworthiness, one of the important issues raised is that of authority. Who decided which books should be included in the Bible as the authoritative Word of God, and why should we accept their word for it? I have heard the objection phrased in the following way: 'Hundreds of years after the events, a group of men got together and decided what should be in the Bible. Why should I accept that?' In our twenty-first-century, postmodern context, when questions of power and authority are so inter-twined with questions about meaning, the process of compilation of a text is of increasing importance.

Let us begin by defining our terms. The word 'canon' comes from the Greek word *kanon*, meaning 'reed'. The reed was used as a measuring rod and has connotations of a standard or a fixed measuring point. The word 'canon' applied to Scripture means 'a limited and defined group of writings which are accepted as authoritative within the Christian Church'.[1] But did a group of men just randomly decide which books were in and which were out?

The New Testament canon

The New Testament is made up of twenty-seven books, many of which were written as letters by the apostles to the different congregations of the early church. There are also four Gospels, which are historical accounts based on eyewitness testimony about the events surrounding the life, death and resurrection of the historical person, Jesus Christ. The Acts of the Apostles is a historical account of the very beginnings of the church, and it details the lives and journeys of the first apostles who took Christianity to the world. The book of Revelation is the account of an intriguing vision which the Apostle John had whilst he was exiled on the island of Patmos at the end of his life.

During the lifetime of the apostles the church grew at a phenomenal rate and spread over the breadth of the Mediterranean world. Across Europe, Asia and Africa the church was flourishing and growing during the first four centuries after Christianity's inception. The different books of the New Testament as we have it today were copied and reproduced throughout the spread of the church. This was encouraged by the writers of the New Testament – Paul tells the Colossians to make sure the Laodicean church reads his letter too (Colossians 4:16), and he encourages the Thessalonians to let the epistle be 'read to all the brothers' (1 Thessalonians 5:27). The early records show that everywhere the church spread, the contents of the New Testament were known and reproduced, which meant that a Christian could travel from Rome to Alexandria or from Alexandria to Ephesus and be welcomed as a brother or sister. Letters were the means of communication between the distant churches, and there are many examples of such letters: Clement of Rome wrote to the church in Corinth, and Ignatius wrote to various churches on the eve of his martyrdom. The wide circulation of the New Testament and the sheer numbers of churches involved in reading and propagating it acted as a protection against forgery and fraud, as any interloper would have had to convince large numbers of people across a vast geographical area.

The churches preserved the writings of the apostles and the Gospels from the very time of the apostles' presence in their midst, whilst the letters and books were being written. The fact that these were then so widely made known and multiplied meant that one part of the church could act as a check and balance with another, making forgeries unlikely. The communion of the different parts of the church with each other meant that mistakes and frauds could be guarded against.

The manuscript tradition of the New Testament is preserved in great numbers from different places around the globe. We have distinct streams of manuscripts which come to us now from the time of the events they record and preserved in different languages – the same text of the New Testament with minor differences in spellings and occasionally different words. This wealth of manuscript material constitutes independent witnesses for the same text, existing in different parts of the world. The books which are preserved in this way are the canonical books of the New Testament. There are versions in Latin, Greek, Syriac, Coptic, Sahidic, Arabic, Ethiopic, Armenian and many other languages.

So the books of the New Testament were widely known throughout the world church and different sections were read out in church services each week. Justin Martyr (AD 110–65) wrote:

> On the day called Sunday there is a gathering together to one place of all those who live in cities or in the country and the memoirs of the apostles or the writings of the prophets are read as long as time permits . . . [2]

It seems that Christians began to collect the writings of the apostles and evangelists of the church from an early date and very soon began to treat them as authoritative and scriptural. Already by the end of the first century AD, Clement, Bishop of Rome, writes to the church in Corinth and quotes from Paul's letter to the Corinthians as though it had binding authority similar to that of the Old Testament. Justin Martyr quotes from the Gospels, beginning his citations with the important formula, 'It is written', recognizing their scriptural authority.

The writings of the early church Fathers also refer to the various books of the New Testament as Scripture in the early church. Eusebius (who was born in AD 270) mentions the various books of the New Testament. His work is interesting because he distinguishes three categories of writings:

1. Books universally acknowledged (*homolegoumena*) as scriptural.
2. Books whose scriptural status is disputed by some (*antilegoumena*).
3. Books which should be rejected as spurious (*notha*).

The second category is interesting because it includes James, Jude, 2 Peter, 2 and 3 John and Revelation as books which were disputed by some. Revelation is seen as a special case because many thought of it as universally acknowledged, whilst some in the Eastern churches raised questions about it. However, the rest of the New Testament fitted into category one – universally acknowledged as Scripture. Eusebius does mention some heretical literature which was acknowledged as false by the church, and he names works such as *Shepherd* by Hermas and the *Epistle of Barnabas*. It is interesting that most of the New Testament was regarded by all the churches as being authoritative and scriptural by this point. It is important for us to grasp here that although lists appear in the writings of the church Fathers, Christians did not begin to regard the various books they mentioned as authoritative simply because an individual like Eusebius decreed that they were. The Gospels and all the other *homolegoumena* were exactly that – agreed by all already. One scholar usefully comments:

> The recognition of the books of the New Testament as
> scriptural was overwhelmingly a natural process, not a matter
> of ecclesiastical regulation. The core of the New Testament

was accepted so early that subsequent rulings do no more than recognise the obvious.[3]

Where there were question-marks, these were dealt with openly. With the letter of James there were questions about authorship, and yet there was strong reason to believe that the writer was James the son of Zebedee or James the brother of Jesus – both were apostles in the New Testament church. In further support of the letter of James is the fact of its inclusion in the Syriac version, as the church of Syria bordered on Palestine, where James the brother of Jesus was a bishop. Eusebius tells us that this epistle was widely received by the great majority of Christians. With the epistle to the Hebrews, questions were raised as to its authorship, but again, it was in the Syriac canon and was mentioned by many of the church Fathers and councils, and was finally included in the canon.

On the whole the New Testament books made their way into the church naturally and were accepted from the time they were written by the apostles and evangelists in the church across the world. Those books that were questioned did not come to final acceptance or rejection because of a fiat by a group of powerful men – rather, a consensus emerged in the church either recognizing authority or rejecting it.

The church Father Athanasius wrote a letter to his clergy in AD 367, and his list is identical to our canon:

Again it is not tedious to speak of the books of the New Testament. These are the four gospels, according to Matthew, Mark, Luke and John. Afterwards the Acts of the Apostles and Epistles (called Catholic), seven viz. of James, one; of Peter, two; of John, three; after these one of Jude. In addition, there are fourteen Epistles of Paul, written in this order. The first, to the Romans; then two to the Corinthians; after these, to the Galatians; next to the Ephesians, then to the Philippians; then to the Colossians; after these, two to the Thessalonians, and that to the Hebrews; and again, two to Timothy; one to

Titus; and lastly that to Philemon. And besides the Revelation of John . . . [4]

When thinking or talking about the canon, the important concept to remember is that the church did not *choose* the canon; rather, it officially recognized the inspiration of certain books. As we have seen, the inspiration of the twenty-seven books of the New Testament was already generally accepted in the early church, and when a council of church leaders met in AD 393 in Hippo and then again in 397 in Carthage, it was to confirm this and to counteract early heresies and persecution. As F. F. Bruce writes:

> When at last a Church Council – the Synod of Hippo in
> AD 393 – listed the twenty-seven books of the New Testament,
> it did not confer upon them any authority which they did not
> already possess, but simply recorded their previously
> established canonicity.[5]

One of the reasons for this meeting of a church council was the increasing challenge of heresies spreading with the growing distance in time from the period when the New Testament was written. The most serious heretical challenge came from Marcion, who lived around AD 140. He distinguished between an inferior creator God of the Old Testament and God the Father revealed in Christ. He argued that the church should jettison all that pointed to the former. He wanted to expunge anything hinting at Judaism in the Bible. When this and other heretical teachings began to pose serious challenges, it became important for the church to have explicit parameters within which to work.

The Old Testament canon

Although the question about the canon raised by a sceptical non-Christian is usually referring to the New Testament, it is interesting to examine the Old Testament too. This is made a little more difficult by the inclusion in the Roman Catholic Bible of a group of writings called the Apocrypha. The fact that Christ and the apostles constantly refer to the Old Testament as the Scriptures forms the foundation for Christians believing in the Jewish Old Testament as an integral part of the Word of God. Jesus says in John 5:39, 'These are the Scriptures that testify about me . . . ' and he constantly addresses the Jewish people as if they have the Scriptures. So we must ask ourselves – what are these Scriptures to which Jesus is referring? The evidence points towards an established Hebrew canon before 150 BC. Josephus (born in AD 37) tells us that a copy of the Hebrew Scriptures was preserved in the temple. He categorizes the Old Testament as the Law, the Prophets and other books which he calls 'hymns and instructions for men's lives' (or the Hagiographa). He informs us that the Jews have twenty-two books in their Bible, corresponding to the number of letters in the Hebrew alphabet. This was organized by the two books of Samuel being counted as one, as were the two books of Kings, Ezra and Nehemiah, Jeremiah and Lamentations, Judges and Ruth respectively. He counted the five books of the Pentateuch as the Law, thirteen books as the Prophets and four as the Hagiographa. Josephus does not include the Apocrypha in his description of the canon of the Old Testament. Neither did the Christian church during the first four centuries of its life. In fact, many church Fathers, including Jerome, the great scholar and translator of the Latin Vulgate, spoke out against the inclusion of the Apocrypha in the Old Testament. He argued that the church could read these books 'for example of life and instruction of manners' but he does not 'apply them to establish any doctrine'.[6]

The Thirty-nine Articles of the Church of England picked up this approach. It was not until 1546, in a polemical action by the Counter-Reformation Council of Trent, that the Roman Catholic Church gave full canonical status to the Apocrypha. Furthermore, the canon of the Old Testament without the Apocrypha was discussed by Jewish scholars at Jamnia in AD 90, and this is the Old Testament that the early church assented to.

The main point to remember here as we examine the canon of the Old and New Testaments and ask how the Bible came to be as it is today, is that the authority of the Bible was not dependent upon councils of men choosing its books. The canon was widely accepted within the church as authoritative and scriptural, but because of attacks on the integrity of the church and the growth of the church geographically, it became important to have the books of the Bible publicly recognized by a central agency so that unity could be preserved.

6 What about the other holy books?

So far you may agree that the Bible is reliable, that it can convey some meaning beyond the reader's own bias, or that it may give us access to historical events. But many people go on to wonder what is so unique about the Bible. Aren't the Muslim scriptures or the Hindu Vedas just as reliable and accurate? What makes the Bible any better than them? Why should I choose to believe it rather than any other holy book?

Many people believe that all the religions in the world are basically the same but with a few superficial differences. This is a popular view which is repeated time and time again. However, the reality is quite the opposite. Pantheistic Hinduism and Buddhism believe that there is no personal God, only an Ultimate impersonal reality. Polytheistic Hinduism believes in 330 million personal gods and goddesses. Islam and Judaism believe in one God, and Christianity believes in a Trinitarian God who is one and three. As the poet Steve Turner wrote in his poem 'The Atheist's Creed':

> We believe there is something in horoscopes, UFOs and bent spoons.

Jesus was a good man just like Buddha, Mohammed and ourselves.

We believe he was a good teacher of morals but we believe that his good morals are really bad.

We believe that all religions are basically the same, at least the one we read was, they all believe in love and goodness, they only differ on matters of creation, sin, heaven, hell, God and salvation.[1]

The style, authorship and content of the holy books that we come across in the different religions of the world are incredibly diverse, and a mature approach from a seeker of truth will quickly reveal this. In this chapter we are going to look at the Bible in relation to the Muslim Qur'an and the Hindu Vedas.

Islam

We only need to look at the news to realize that huge tensions exist between Islam and people of other faiths in the world today. Whether we are talking about the blowing up of the Buddhas in Afghanistan by the Taliban[2] or the tension between Muslims and Hindus in India and Kashmir, we see that there are major differences between the world religions. The Islamic critique of Mel Gibson's film *The Passion of the Christ* has been a deeply felt objection to any presentation of the death of Jesus by crucifixion. BBC Radio 4's programme *The Moral Maze* was discussing this film and whether it might stir up anti-Semitism. The Islamic expert made clear that his only real concern about the film was that it depicted Jesus dying, and Muslims do not believe that Jesus died on the cross.

Situations like this one only serve to underline the reality of different truth claims and the danger of pretending that such differences do not exist. The Qur'an and the Bible are in absolute disagreement on a number of issues, and it is worth understanding this if we are going to come to any conclusions for ourselves about truth.

Muhammad, the founder of Islam

Muhammad was born around AD 570 and we know about his history from the *Hadith* – anecdotes about his life which were collected after his death. The holy book of Islam is the Qur'an, and it is believed to be the final revelation of Allah (God) to human beings. It comes to us through the final prophet of Islam – Muhammad. His place in Islamic thinking is one of high honour. He is presented in the Qur'an as a mere human being but the most elevated human who will ever live. Prophethood itself is seen as the height of Allah's activity in the world, and so to be the last and greatest of all prophets was the most significant honour which could be given by God to a human. One *hadith* demonstrates Muhammad's view of himself:

> I have been granted excellence over the other prophets in six things: the earth has been made a mosque for me, with its soil declared pure; booty has been made lawful for me; I have been given victory through the inspiring awe at the distance of a month's journey; I have been given permission to intercede; I have been sent to all mankind; and the prophets have been sealed with me.[3]

How did Muhammad 'receive' the Qur'an? He was in the habit of going away to a secluded place on Mount Hira to think and pray for one month of each year. This was in accordance with local pagan customs. On one such occasion, when he was around the age of forty, he had a dream that the Angel Gabriel appeared to him and taught him some words which now appear in the 96th Sura of the Qur'an. The rest of the Qur'an came to him over a period of about twenty-two years in different places and contexts.

Although Muhammad is not considered divine in orthodox Islam, the honour given to him by many Muslims goes beyond the bounds of the Qur'an. One important example of this is the popular tradition that Muhammad will act as an intercessor on judgment day. There are thousands of Islamic poems and prayers which express the hope that Muhammad's intercession will win salvation for the writer.

The prophets

The Islamic view is that in successive generations Allah revealed himself through prophets. These human beings were men of good character who were chosen to convey a divine message in particular contexts. The Muslim conviction is that each of these prophets, although raised up at different times and in different communities, all had the same basic message. This message was to call people to believe in the oneness of God, to submit to his law and do good works with the judgment of God in mind.

The Qur'an

Muslims believe that the Qur'an is the final revelation of God to human beings and that it comes through the final prophet of Islam – Muhammad. In the text of the Qur'an the prophets who came before him are alluded to; indeed, many biblical names are mentioned, as are various Arabian reformers from neighbouring vicinities. However, the supremacy of the revelation of the Qur'an is consistently emphasized, as is the supremacy of the prophet who received the revelations. This means that Muhammad and his revelations are believed to be superior to Jesus and any revelation that Christians believe is contained in the Bible.

The Qur'an on other holy books

In the early period of Muhammad's ministry he declared that the Torah (the Old Testament) and the Gospels were acceptable for Muslims: 'Say, O People of the Book! You have naught of guidance till you observe the Torah and the Gospel and that which was revealed unto you from your Lord' (Sura 5:68). In fact, Muhammad is himself commanded to look at these scriptures when in doubt: 'So, if thou art in doubt regarding what We have sent down to thee, ask those who recite the Book before thee' (Sura 10:95). However, this raises some interesting historical questions for the Christian. Muslims have claimed that the Gospels, known as the *Injil*, have been corrupted and changed. These Gospels, in their original form, used to agree with what Muhammad said about Jesus only being a prophet and not God, but they have been changed by Christians to make statements about the divinity and supremacy of Christ. The influential Muslim commentator Yusuf Ali comments that the *Injil* mentioned in the Qur'an is certainly not the New Testament and it is not the four Gospels as now received by the Christian church, but an original gospel which was given by Jesus, just as the Torah was promulgated by Moses and the Qur'an by Muhammad (Sura 2:86).

There are a number of problems with this basic assertion, the most obvious of which is that there is simply no way of verifying that there is some earlier gospel. Also, Muhammad himself does not refer to an earlier unchanged book, and the extant early manuscript tradition of the New Testament makes it highly implausible that an even earlier, entirely different manuscript tradition exists somewhere. The Pentateuch and the four Gospels as we have them today were in existence during the time of Muhammad and for a long time before.[4] Nowhere in the Qur'an itself is it stated that Christians, known as 'People of the Book', did not possess the authentic Scriptures, and neither does the Qur'an itself claim that the *Injil* had been corrupted by Christians. The statement is made now because Muhammad's versions of various biblical events differ from what we find in the texts of the Old and New Testaments. This is an important point, because it is only later Islamic tradition which rejects the Bible, not the Qur'an itself.

Islam and Judaism

In his ministry Muhammad was, at first, sympathetic towards the Jews. In the early Meccan passages of the Qur'an he commends all 'People of the Book', as he hoped that he would be accepted as their long-awaited prophet:

> Dispute not with the People of the Book save in the fairer
> manner, except for those of them that do wrong; and say,
> 'We believe in what has been sent down to us, and what has
> been sent down to you; and God and your God is One, and
> to Him we have surrendered.'
> (Sura 29:45)

As time went by, the Arabian Jews and Christians increasingly rejected Muhammad as a false prophet, and his growing
frustration is reflected in the Qur'an. From his initially friendly
comments, he turns to condemnation of those who have rejected
him as an inauthentic prophet: 'Whoso desires another religion
than Islam, it shall not be accepted of him; in the next world
he shall be among the losers' (Sura 3:79–80). This attitude is
reflected not only in his pronouncements about the afterlife
but also in his increasingly sour words on the earthly relationships between the different communities of the 'People of the
Book'. In Sura 9:29 the seeds of conflict against the Jews are
sown:

> Fight those who believe not in God and the Last Day and do
> not forbid what God and His Messenger have forbidden –
> such men practise not the religion of truth, being of those
> who have been given the Book – until they pay the tribute
> out of hand and have been humbled.

The Qur'an explains this change of attitude towards the Jews in
particular as a response to the rejection of prophets and messengers throughout history:

> So, for their breaking the compact, and disbelieving in the
> signs of God, and slaying the Prophets without the right, and
> for their saying, 'Our hearts are uncircumcised' – nay, but
> God sealed them for their unbelief, so they believe not.
> (Sura 4:154)

The Qur'an and Old Testament history

The Qur'an retells various stories from the Old Testament but subtly changes some of the details. For example, Haman is a minister of Pharaoh in Sura 40:36, and Ezra is referred to as if Jews believed he was the son of God in Sura 9:30. The differences between Qur'anic accounts and biblical accounts are not unimportant or minor. The Qur'an contains confusions of the original stories as recorded in the older biblical texts. Mohammad gives no reason for changing these details of the stories he alludes to. Islamic scholars insist that the Bible must have been corrupted because it undermines the Qur'an's grasp of history. However, this is arguing backwards from the assumption that the Qur'an is true. The historical and manuscript *evidence* points in the opposite direction, strongly affirming the Jewish and Christian texts as the more accurate and reliable recordings of historical events.

The text of the Qur'an

Muhammad did not write down his revelations but preached them and passed them on orally. Because of this, after Muhammad's death, it became increasingly important that the scattered pieces of revelation be gathered into a coherent whole which could be used by the growing Muslim community. The process of compiling the Qur'an is recorded by Islamic tradition. According to this tradition, Muhammad received the different passages of the Qur'an verbatim from the angel Gabriel over a period of twenty-three years (Suras 25:32; 17:106). Having received the words, Muhammad would then recite them to the community, who in turn memorized them. Scribes would copy down the words onto scraps of paper, stones, palm leaves or bits of leather. These pieces of writing were then collected together by Zayd ibn Thabit, one of Muhammad's trusted scribes. This is described in the *Hadith*:

Then Abu Bakr said, 'You are a wise young man and we do not have any suspicion about you, and you used to write the Divine Inspiration for Allah's Apostle. So you should search

for the Qur'an and collect it' ... So I started looking for the
Qur'an and collecting it from palm-leaf stalks, thin white
stones and also from the men who knew it by heart.[5]

However, it came to the attention of 'Uthman, the third Muslim
Caliph, that different Islamic communities were using slightly
different versions of the Qur'an. Zayd was again chosen to oversee
the project of confirming the authoritative version of the Qur'an.
Again the *Hadith* records what happened:

'Uthman sent a message to Hafsa saying, 'Send us the
manuscripts of the Qur'an so that we may compile the
Qur'anic materials in perfect copies and return the
manuscripts to you.' Hafsa sent it to 'Uthman. 'Uthman
then ordered Zaid bin Thabit, 'abdullah bin Az-Zubair, Sa'id
bin Al-As, and 'Abdur-Rahman bin Harith bin Hisham to
rewrite the manuscripts in perfect copies ... When they had
written many copies, 'Uthman returned the original manuscript to Hafsa. 'Uthman sent to every Muslim province one
copy of what they had copied, and ordered that all the other
Qur'anic materials whether written in fragmentary
manuscripts or whole copies be burnt.[6]

There is disagreement between academics over the precise details
of the textual development of the Qur'an. However, scholars
agree that the 'Uthmanic version of the Qur'an has remained
intact through to the present day.

When compared with the text of the Old and New Testaments,
there has been relatively little scholarly critique of the manuscripts
or literary form of the Qur'an. However, discovery of some ancient
Qur'anic fragments in Yemen in 1972 has led to increasing research
into the textual development of the Qur'an in recent years. Gerd-R.
Puin, a specialist in Arabic calligraphy and Qur'anic paleography
based at Saarland University in Saarbrücken, Germany, has been
examining the Yemeni fragments since 1981. His findings reveal

unconventional verse orderings, minor textual variations, and some artistic embellishment. Among the manuscripts were some palimpsests or versions which had clearly been written over even earlier, and had then been washed off. What the Yemeni Qur'ans seemed to suggest was an *evolving* text. Since the early 1980s more than 15,000 sheets of the Yemeni Qur'ans have painstakingly been flattened, cleaned, treated, sorted and assembled; they now sit in Yemen's House of Manuscripts, awaiting detailed examination. In 1997 the task of taking more than 35,000 microfilm pictures of the fragments was finished, and now scholars will be able to scrutinize the texts and publish their findings freely. Andrew Rippon has commented:

> The impact of the Yemeni manuscripts is still to be felt ...
> Their variant readings and verse orders are all very
> significant. Everybody agrees on that. These manuscripts
> say that the early history of the Qur'anic text is much more
> of an open question than many have suspected: the text was
> less stable, and therefore had less authority, than has always
> been claimed.[7]

Literary style

There are no miracles related to Muhammad's life, but Muslims claim that the self-authenticating miracle in Islam is the Qur'an. The Qur'an is written in Arabic poetry and prose, and the Islamic faith considers the very language of the Qur'an to be totally unique. The book itself is held to be perfect, dictated by God and the ultimate expression of truth. The Iranian Islamic scholar Sayyid Hossein Nasr comments: 'Many people, especially non-Muslims, who read the Qur'an for the first time are struck by what appears to be a kind of incoherence from the human point of view. It is neither like a high mystical text nor a manual of Aristotelian logic, though it contains both mysticism and logic.' He then goes on to say, 'The Qur'an contains a quality which is difficult to express in modern language. One might call it divine magic.'[8] However, it is very difficult to maintain that a written text is perfect. The Iranian author Ali Dashti commented in his book *Twenty-Three Years: The Life of the Prophet Mohammed* that the errors in the Qur'an were so many that the grammatical rules of Arabic had to be altered in order to fit the claim that the book was perfect.

Interpretation

Interpretation of the Qur'an is a complex issue within the world-wide and historical spectrum of Islam. A good starting place for understanding Islamic interpretation is the belief that any 'translation' of the text from Arabic into another language robs the Qur'an of its divine authenticity. Any attempt to translate the Qur'an from Arabic is therefore seen merely as an interpretation and not a copy of the holy book itself. This is problematic for anyone who is interested in discovering more about Islam but has not been born into a Muslim home. Theoretically, if one does not have the intellectual capacity, education or inclination to learn ancient Arabic, one cannot actually read the Qur'an or appreciate the main miracle and self-authenticating aspect of Islam.

A number of specific schools of interpretation have developed over the centuries as Muslims wrestled with applying the text in their communities.[9] The Qur'an has increasingly been read through the lenses of these schools. Divisions between Muslims over what the Qur'an means have occurred when various sects have sought to abandon the interpretive framework laid down by centuries of scholars. Reforming movements have sought to get back to the 'original' meaning of the text, unfettered by the layers of human guidelines and traditions which had built up. Because of the inflammatory nature of some of the suras of the Qur'an, these reforming groups have been inspired to take drastic action.

The difficulty of dialogue with Muslims is a challenge for all seekers of truth. Whilst Muslims feel free to impugn the most precious of Christian beliefs, such as the deity of Christ, and the most sacred Jewish beliefs, such as the revealed Torah, anyone who asks questions about the character or reliability of Muhammad or the Qur'an is reviled as a blasphemer.

The uniqueness of the Bible

The Bible stands in stark contrast to the Qur'an in a number of ways. The Bible does not claim to be dictation given by God. In fact, it is unashamedly open about human participation in its pages. It was written by a variety of authors, many of whom are named, across a time-span of a couple of thousand years. It is a holy book inspired by God and also involving human collaboration. How could we humans read, know or understand something completely divine, totally 'other'? Such a book would be inaccessible to us. The Bible is *revelation* from God which connects with us – we human beings are capable of reading, understanding and appreciating it because the message comes through human messengers. It is divine and inspired and, what is more, it is communicated in a way we can access.

The Bible contains reliable accounts of the life, ministry and death of Jesus. These Gospels were not written by Jesus himself. They were written by and from the testimony of those who knew him intimately. They were written in the lifetimes of those who knew him and witnessed how he lived and died. The historicity of the events recorded in the Bible is open to scrutiny and question, and some of these events can be cross-referenced with other historical source material. For example, in contrast to the Qur'an, Josephus claimed that 'Pilatus condemned him to the cross' (*Antiquities*, XVIII.63–64). The Babylonian Talmud states that 'on the eve of the Passover they hanged Yeshua of Nazareth' (43a). Tacitus (a Roman historian) and Lucian (a second-century Greek satirist) both maintained that Jesus was crucified.

The Bible refers to events, setting them in historical, geographical and chronological contexts. We are expected to recognize these events in their historical context – they truly happened. The

Bible was not written as myth. The details around the events are given so that, through the centuries, future generations might know that the biblical accounts are not mere glosses of other literature cobbled together in the mind of an individual. They are intended as sensible, truthful accounts of events. They are often given with an interpretation, but the interpretation is not every-thing – enough facts and details are supplied to give us access to the events themselves.

The Bible and the Qur'an, then, are quite different in their composition, intention, historical referencing, and openness to translation and scrutiny. How does all of this compare with the holy writings of Hinduism?

Hinduism

Hinduism is an incredibly complex and diverse religion, and it is difficult to avoid simplification if we are to bring it within manage-able and understandable proportions. For our purposes in this chapter, I want to take a brief look at the Hindu scriptures rather than attempt a comprehensive description of the Hindu religion.

The total mass of writings comprising the Hindu scriptures is truly vast. Within the corpus of writings considered to be divinely revealed is a group of books called the Vedas which are accepted by Hindus as sacred. The Vedas (the name means 'sacred knowledge') comprise four *samhitas*, collections of hymns written in ancient Sanskrit.[10] The date and place of their composition has been the subject of much scholarly dispute. Indian tradition dates the Vedas to around 4000 BC and assumes a north-west Indian origin. Western scholars since Max Muller[11] have assumed a date of 1500–1200 BC, and consider the writings to have been authored by Aryan invaders of India from southern Russia. The texts were transmitted orally for over 1,000 years and the earliest available Sanskrit writings on which Hinduism is based can be dated to 150 BC.

The Vedas were transmitted orally but the necessary learning and recitation was only authorized for Brahmins. Strangers and low-caste people were forbidden from hearing or speaking the scriptures. The initial distinctions between the Aryan and non-Aryan people on the basis of colour (*varna*) evolved into the order of caste hierarchy which still survives in India today. The social classes of the Aryan people – priest, warrior, merchant – assumed the position of the three 'twice-born' high castes of *Brahmin*, *Kshatriya* and *Vaishya*. The term *Dasa*, meaning 'slave', was given to the indigenous people of the subcontinent. These and those born of mixed parentage became the 'once-born' *Shudra* lower peasant caste. Many of the indigenous people had to flee into the forests and hills for fear of their lives after the invasion, and those who fled were later to become the Untouchables.

The Hindu scriptures are such a huge collection of writings that we do not have space to analyse them in any great detail – the *Rig Veda* alone consists of 1,017 hymns divided into 10 books with an appendix of 11 poems.

It is important to note that the Vedas are not historical documents in the same sense as the Old and New Testaments. They record outbursts of praise to various gods as well as mythical stories. It is not clear from the writings themselves whether the events recorded are intended to be understood as historical or imaginary. A number of Hindu thinkers are themselves candid about this. Swami Vivekananda pointed out that Vedic scriptures make mention of a number of Krishnas. It does not matter which is which – the possibility of a legendary mix-up is allowed by him.[12] There is no clear intention of conveying historical truth.

The dating of the various and diverse Hindu scriptures is also a challenging prospect. Writing about this, one scholar comments: 'In spite of claims made by some, in reality, any dating of these documents that attempts a precision closer than a few centuries is as stable as a house of cards.'[13] The contrast with the Bible is very clear here. Through successive generations different books of the Old and New Testaments were written in their historical contexts.

These contexts can be scrutinized and the archaeological and extra-biblical sources from the same times can be placed alongside the biblical writings. The Bible is clear, in talking about itself, that God reveals himself through these different writers at different times, but they all point forwards to the coming of his Son: 'In the past God spoke to our forefathers through the prophets at many times and in various ways, but in these last days he has spoken to us by his Son' (Hebrews 1:1–2).

The Christian message is unique and clear: God not only spoke through human beings, inspiring them to write down historical events and prophetic messages. He himself came. Jesus Christ walked on this earth so that human beings could know God come to be with us. In the New Testament we have reliable accounts of what it was like to be with this Jesus: 'We have seen his glory, the glory of the One and Only' (John 1:14). But more than that, we are invited into personal relationship with this God. As Jesus walks off the pages of Scripture, we can know him, and through the Holy Spirit dwelling in our hearts, we can have vibrant and dynamic relationship with God in the here and now.

7 Isn't the Bible sexist?

Today there is a widespread belief around that the Bible is some kind of powerful patriarchal conspiracy which has been used to oppress women. As a female speaker, I find that this question frequently comes: 'How can you, as a woman, promote such a sexist book? The church has tried to keep women down!' Even as I have been writing this chapter, I have had two such conversations with women outside of the faith for whom this question looms large. It is important, as with other questions, to realize that there could be all kinds of circumstances and experiences behind a question like this. The Christian should be sensitive to the issues which underlie such an emotive question. While it may indeed seem to be the case that women have been discriminated against by religion, the Bible itself deserves closer examination on the subject. What does the text itself have to say about this matter? How is it that many of the greatest Jewish and Christian pioneers have been women – Florence Nightingale, Elizabeth Fry, the Suffragettes, Catherine Booth, Rosa Luxemburg and Ernestine Rose – to name but a few. What does the Bible really say about this subject?

Throughout the Bible there are numerous positive images of women and stories which involve women. In the Old Testament women share the image of God at creation. At the end of time at the Second Coming of Jesus, the church is represented as the bride of Christ. Right the way through, from beginning to end, the Bible includes the feminine as an integral part of the Judaeo-Christian tradition. While it is true that the Bible was written over a long period of time in specific cultures, and some of these contexts did not give equal social advantages to women, it would not be true to say that the message of the Bible is sexist or discriminatory against women.

Women in the New Testament

In the New Testament there are quite a number of significant events involving women – particularly considering the conservative cultural attitudes of the context in which it was written. This context is opened up to our view by a simple statement in John's Gospel in the famous encounter between Jesus and the Samaritan woman at the well (chapter 4). There is a telling little sentence in verse 27 which sheds a great deal of light on just how radical the Bible is in affirming women. The disciples come across Jesus during his conversation with the woman and we are told they 'were surprised to find him talking with a woman'. This is the context of Jesus' ministry, and yet he goes against these cultural trends time and time again.

He does this firstly by having female disciples. In a culture where the idea of women travelling around with a group of men or having the status of disciple was seriously questionable, a number of women are included in Jesus' travelling circle:

The Twelve were with him, and also some women who had been cured of evil spirits and diseases: Mary (called Magdalene) from whom seven demons had come out; Joanna

the wife of Chuza, the manager of Herod's household;
Susanna; and many others. These women were helping
to support them out of their own means.
(Luke 8:1–3)

By mentioning these women by name, the tradition offers praise
and gratitude to them for their financial contributions to the
ministry of Jesus. A sharp contrast may be seen here with authors
such as Ben Sirach of Jerusalem (c. 195 BC), who reflect a more
prevalent attitude of the time with statements such as: 'Bad
temper, insolence and shame hold sway where the wife supports
the husband' (Sir. 25:22). In Matthew 12:46–50, when Jesus is told
that his mother and brothers are waiting outside to see him, he
points to his disciples and says, 'Here are my mother and my
brothers.' This statement is unthinkable unless there were women
among his disciples. In the Middle Eastern culture of the first
century it would be unspeakably offensive to point to male
disciples and use female imagery to describe them.

We also see Jesus teaching women in the New Testament. In
Luke 10:38 we read of Mary, who sits at the feet of Jesus and
engages in theological study, much to her sister's chagrin. This
phrase, 'to sit at the feet of', is the same formulation as in Acts
22:3, where Paul describes his training under Gamaliel. The clear
implication here is that Mary is affirmed as worthy of a rabbi's
theological instruction. Indeed, it is interesting that in John's
Gospel we read that Martha, Mary's sister, is the first person to be
taught one of the most astounding theological statements of the
New Testament. Jesus says to her, 'I am the resurrection and
the life. He who believes in me will live, even though he dies'
(John 11:25). The Mishnah, a collection of Jewish writings, says: 'If
any man gives his daughter a knowledge of the Law it is as though
he taught her lechery.'[1] In contrast to the cultural norms of the
time, Jesus made a habit of revealing great theological truths to
women. The first person who discovers Christ's true identity in
John's Gospel is the Samaritan woman at the well (John 4:25–26):

'The woman said, "I know that Messiah" (called Christ) "is coming. When he comes, he will explain everything to us." Then Jesus declared, "I who speak to you am he." ' We must not underestimate how radical this is – Jesus was turning cultural taboos on their heads by teaching women and allowing them to be his disciples.

Not only does Jesus act in a counter-cultural manner which affirms the feminine, he also teaches and speaks about women in a new and fresh way. His parables are drawn from the life experience of both men and women. For example, the parable of mending the garment – an everyday image from the female sphere – is coupled with the parable of making the wine – an everyday image from the male sphere (Luke 5:36–39). In Matthew 5:14–15 Jesus takes the image of light and then uses a metaphor from the world of men to do with building a city, and a metaphor from the world of women to do with lighting lamps in the home. But he goes further than this in his teaching – he actually portrays God in feminine form. In Luke 15 Jesus follows a parable about a shepherd searching for a lost sheep with a parable about a woman searching for a lost coin. God is depicted as a woman down on her hands and knees, searching through her house for a coin. This passage follows on from Jesus' statement likening himself to a mother hen: 'O Jerusalem, Jerusalem, you who kill the prophets and stone those sent to you, how often I have longed to gather your children together, as a hen gathers her chicks under her wings' (Luke 13:34). Not only does Jesus teach women theology, he also uses feminine imagery in his parables; but he goes further even than this when he speaks of God using feminine language and imagery.

Following on from this, we see that women played an important and prominent role as historic witnesses to the central events surrounding Jesus Christ. It was a group of women who stood at the foot of the cross, watching Jesus die and hearing his last words, and it was a group of women who first witnessed the resurrection of Christ. Again, it is striking for us to remember that the word of women was perceived as having less value than that of men. It is therefore enormously important that the most significant events of Jesus' death and resurrection were witnessed at first hand primarily by women.

When we go on to look at the place of women in the early church, we see that the New Testament ascribes numerous different roles to them. We have women as teachers of theology – an example of which comes in Acts 18:24–26 where Apollos is taught by a couple called Priscilla and Aquila. Apollos is a famous and eloquent preacher and Priscilla team-teaches with her husband. It is unusual to see a woman's name appearing first – as if to emphasize that she had a very real teaching role in this circumstance.

Luke's Gospel presents Mary as a teacher of theology, ethics and social justice for the whole church when he records the Magnificat for us. We also have women presented as deacons. Romans 16:1–2 introduces Phoebe as a deacon of the church. The Greek has the masculine form *diakonon* – Phoebe is a deacon, not a deaconess. One writer comments: 'We regard it as virtually certain that Phoebe is being described as "a" or possibly "the" deacon of the church in question, and that this occurrence of *diakonos* is to be classified with its occurrences in Philippians 1:1 and 1 Timothy 3:8 and 12.'[2] This title in its male form is probably given to Phoebe as the formal title for the clearly defined role of deacon. This title is given elsewhere to Timothy, who led a church in Ephesus, as well as to Apollos and the apostle Paul himself. Furthermore, Phoebe is described as being *prostatis* over many and Paul himself. This word *prostatis* occurs only here in the New Testament, but in the Greek literature of the time it can be translated as 'leader', 'ruler', 'protector' or 'president'.[3] One Greek lexicon denotes *prostatis* as referring to 'governor, chieftain, president and someone in charge of a temple'.[4] Paul seems to be strongly affirming the ministry of a woman here.

Women are also prophets in the New Testament, exercising this key public ministry role in the early church. We see this in the reference to Philip the evangelist, who 'had four unmarried daughters who had the gift of prophecy' (Acts 21:8–9). We also see Paul giving advice as to the manner in which women are to prophesy in church (see 1 Corinthians 11:4–5). Whatever we may make of his comments on head covering, it does seem that Paul expected women to prophesy. Prophecy was an important part of the early church. Paul said 'God's household' was 'built on the foundation of the apostles and prophets' (Ephesians 2:19–20). Women were clearly involved in prophecy in the New Testament. There is also some evidence that a woman may have been referred to as an apostle by Paul. This is disputed by many, but it is useful for us to look at the possibility. At the end of Paul's letter to the Roman church he includes a whole section of personal greetings, and there we read, 'Greet Andronicus and Junias, my relatives who have been in prison with me. They are outstanding among the apostles, and they were in Christ before I was' (Romans 16:7). The question is, who are these 'outstanding' apostles? In particular, the name 'Jounian' is interesting – it is an accusative singular of a first-declension Greek noun. This accusative can be either masculine or feminine, and so we do not know what the nominative of this name is.[5] There are two possibilities: the name could be feminine, in which case it is 'Junia'; or it could be masculine, in which case it is 'Junias'. The text either refers to a husband-and-wife team called Andronicus and Junia, as Paul has done a few verses earlier when greeting Priscilla and Aquila; or he is referring to two men, Andronicus and Junias. How should we decide between these two possibilities? The early centuries of the church generally saw this name as referring to a woman. Chrysostom writes:

It was the greatest of honours to be counted a fellow prisoner of Paul's . . . Think what great praise it was to be considered of note among the apostles. These two were of note because of their works and achievements. Think how great the devotion of this woman Junia must have been, that she should be worthy to be called an apostle! But even here Paul does not stop his praise, for they were Christians before he was.[6]

The word 'Jounian' was taken in this text to be a feminine name by Origen, Jerome, Abelard and others. One scholar notes that she is unable to find any Latin commentary on the book of Romans that has this name in the masculine form before the late thirteenth century.[7] The final important factor here is that 'Junias' as a male name is unattested in any Latin or Greek text at any time in history, whilst the name 'Junia' has been found over 250 times.[8] While it is contested by some, it does seem likely that the name 'Jounian' in Paul's letter refers to a woman, in which case at least one woman was recognized as fulfilling the important early church role of an apostle.

It is clear that women played a full and vibrant role in the ministry of Jesus, both in terms of the content and the recipients of his teaching. While this may seem absolutely right and proper in our twenty-first-century context, we must remember how radical this was in first-century Palestine. Jesus intentionally affirmed and included women. We see a continuation of this in the early church, where women undertook various roles, from Lydia and Tabitha to Philip's daughters. It is true that there are two difficult passages in Paul's writing which may seem to go against what has been said here. These passages are 1 Corinthians 14:34, which talks about women being silent, and 1 Timothy 2:12, which tells women to be silent, not to teach. The 1 Corinthians passage needs to be read in its context. Only two chapters earlier Paul has described the manner in which women should behave when publicly giving prophecies. So we can see that Paul, in writing this letter, is trying to deal with a particular situation in which there is a problem with disturbances. One of these disturbances is outbursts by people speaking in tongues; another is a group of women chatting during the service. Paul tells the tongues speakers to keep quiet unless there is an interpretation (verse 28), and he tells the women to keep quiet and not disturb others with their chatting and questions.

The 1 Timothy 2 passage is more controversial and is taken by some to mean that women should not teach or have authority in any church. However, as we have seen, this seems to go against some other teaching of the New Testament, much of which the apostle Paul himself wrote. So while some Christians believe that this passage should be taken to mean that women should not have the position of ultimate authority in a church, this would not mean that women are somehow second-class citizens or worthless; rather, it would be an issue of role. However, many scholars argue that this passage from 1 Timothy must be understood in its geographic and cultural context – the context of Ephesus, where the goddess Artemis was worshipped.[9] It is important for us to remember here that the Bible was written in history, and that the letters of the New Testament had relevance to particular situations as well as having broader relevance to us. In a culture that was far slower to recognize the worth of women, we can see that the Bible is highly counter-cultural on this issue. The apostle Paul, who is often demonized as being sexist, in fact freely ministered alongside women, and the two passages in his writings which are sometimes taken as a blanket denial of female ministry need to be seen in this broader perspective.

None of this is to deny that the God of the Bible is over-whelmingly portrayed in terms of masculine language – as Father, King, Lord, and ultimately, in Christ, he comes as a man. Of course Jesus taught his disciples to pray to God as 'Father' (Luke 11:2) and to baptize nations 'in the name of the Father and of the Son and of the Holy Spirit' (Matthew 28:19). This cannot be entirely culturally conditioned, as God chose which cultures and times in which to reveal himself, and he chose that this revelation should be predominantly masculine. However, it would not be true to say that women are excluded or unequal to men. Both male and female are created in the image of God and, as we have seen, God does use some feminine imagery in his revelation of himself.

Women in the Old Testament

In the Old Testament there are numerous images of women. Some of these are surprising. The primary teaching text describing wifely duties does not conform at all to the stereotype of a disempowered woman. Proverbs 31 describes the 'Wife of Noble Character'. She is a woman who has the confidence of her husband; she works hard running an international business; she gets up early and provides for her family and employees; she owns property and cares for the poor; she clothes her household well and dresses beautifully herself; she is in charge of the home and her children honour her; she fears God and is respected by people in her community.

Women in the Old Testament are often spoken of with dignity and value. After Sarai had over-reacted to the arrogance of her maidservant, Hagar, and had driven her out of the house, the angel of the LORD found the run-away at a well (Genesis 16:7). He said, 'Hagar, servant of Sarai . . . ' It would be easy for us to miss the significance of that address. This is the only instance in many thousands of Ancient Near Eastern texts where a deity, or his messenger, calls a woman by name and thereby invests her with exalted dignity. Hagar is the Old Testament counterpart to the Samaritan woman with whom Jesus talked one on one (John 4). It is interesting that both were women, both were not of Abraham's family, and both were sinners, yet God treated them with compassion, gave them special revelations and bestowed on them unconventional dignity.

In the Old Testament women were sometimes called to be 'prophetesses', God's mouth in the world. Miriam (Exodus 15:20–21) was the first of several who are mentioned, including Deborah (Judges 4:4–7), Isaiah's wife (Isaiah 8:3) and Huldah (2 Kings 22:13–20). Joel 2:28 predicts that, in the last days, the LORD will answer Moses' prayer that all the LORD's people, men and women alike, should become prophets (Numbers 11:29). At Pentecost this prediction is fulfilled.

Huldah plays an important role in worship and ministry in the Old Testament. During the rule of Josiah, those who were repairing the temple found the Book of the Law, which had been neglected during the previous generation. Josiah directed five leaders to seek guidance from God about this book. These leaders went to the married prophetess Huldah to verify the book, rather than going to her famous contemporary, the prophet Jeremiah. One scholar comments:

> That officials from the royal court went to a prophetess relatively unknown with so important a matter is strong indication that in this period of Israel's history there is little if any prejudice against a woman's offering of prophecy. If she had received the gift of prophecy, her words were to be given the same authority as those of men.[10]

Women and men were also equal in prayer. Covenant women prayed directly to God without the priestly mediation of their husbands. For example, when the carnal Jacob defaulted in his responsibility to pray for his barren wife (Genesis 30:1–2), in contrast to his godly forefathers, who prayed for their children and wives (cf. 24:7, 12–15; 25:21), Rachel petitioned God directly, and he listened to her and opened her womb (30:22–24). Barren Hannah also sought dignity and worth through child-bearing. She too went directly to God in prayer, independently from her husband, Elkanah, and the high priest, Eli, both of whom were insensitive to her need.

It is true to say that the Old Testament does also contain stories in which terrible things such as rape or violence occur against women, but these are not condoned. Much of the text of the Old Testament is narrative and not didactic in style. Sometimes the author does not comment to condone or condemn particular incidents – it is an account of what happened and the reader is left to respond. However, we do find that the sufferings of women are empathized with – for example, those who are barren and longing for children, such as Hannah, Sarah or Rebekah, are written of tenderly.

While many of the stories of the Old Testament have central male heroic characters, this is not exclusively the case. Again, we must remember the Ancient Near Eastern context in which these narratives were written in order to appreciate the importance of the stories about women such as Deborah in Judges, Queen Esther who saved her people, or Ruth who becomes an ancestor of David and hence of Jesus.

Perhaps even more striking are the passages of the Old Testament which use feminine imagery to describe God. We have seen that Jesus shocked his listeners by doing this in first-century Palestine, but we also see examples of this in the Old Testament. In Isaiah 42:13–14 God draws an analogy between himself and a warrior, and then between himself and a woman giving birth:

> The LORD will march out like a mighty man,
>   like a warrior he will stir up his zeal;
> with a shout he will raise the battle cry
>   and will triumph over his enemies.
> 'For a long time I have kept silent,
>   I have been quiet and held myself back.
> But now, like a woman in childbirth,
>   I cry out, I gasp and pant . . .'

This is an interesting and graphic portrait of God using earthy language from the realm of female experience. Another example of God ascribing female characteristics to himself comes in Isaiah 66:13: 'As a mother comforts her child, so will I comfort you'.

When we come to the text of the Bible with the issue of sexism in mind, we must be clear that while God is predominantly spoken of with male imagery and ultimately incarnates himself as the man Jesus, this is not to say that women are undermined or undervalued. Some female imagery is used of God, and Jesus constantly affirms the value of women, teaching them and interacting with them as human beings. Both male and female are created in the image of God, and both are so precious that Christ came to the earth to redeem them with his blood shed on the cross.

8 What about all the wars?

I am often asked how I can believe in God when there have been so many wars caused by religion. The implication of this question is that if only people would leave behind their convictions about the existence of a God, the world would be a much better, more peaceful place. Of course, very few people ever reflect on the fact that the very reverse of this was demonstrated in the twentieth century, which saw the rise of the atheistic communist and Nazi ideologies and more killing than the previous nineteen centuries put together.

None of this is to say that religion has not at times been a cause or a significant factor in war. Indeed, Christians should be the first to hold their hands up and say that outrages such as the crusades should never have happened and are certainly not a true reflection of what Jesus came to say and accomplish. In fact, true Christian values at the time of the crusades were voiced by leaders such as Francis of Assisi and John Wycliffe, who roundly condemned any killing or warfare in the name of Christ.

And so we come to look at this subject of war in the context of questions about the Bible. And the question is refined a little more to ask how it is that God could sanction war in the Old Testament and, following on from this, it is asked whether this 'warring God' does not present an insurmountably contradictory face to the God of the New Testament, who seems much more loving and kind.

The first question which usually comes is, 'How could a good God, a God of peace, condone warfare as he does in the Old Testament?' This might be referring to a passage like 1 Chronicles 5:22–23, which says: 'They also took one hundred thousand people captive, and many others fell slain, because the battle was God's.' And then people ask, 'How can God not only condone warfare but command it, even giving instructions as to how war should be fought?' Such instructions are actually given in Deuteronomy 20.

Before we get into trying to answer these questions, the first point to make to someone who is examining the Old Testament as a sceptic is that not everything recorded in the Bible is approved by the Bible. For example, the Bible records the assassination of a man called Eglon; this action is neither condemned nor praised, it is simply relayed to us in Judges 3:17–25. Quite a large proportion of the acts of violence recorded in the Bible would fall into this category. We need to be careful, then, how we read the different accounts of war in the Old Testament. However, it is true to say that some wars are commanded by God – particularly with regard to the nation of Israel taking possession of the land that God gives to them after they are rescued from slavery in Egypt. Christians have deliberated for many generations over how to understand these passages, as well as how to build a Christian response to war in their own contemporary contexts.

I would like to begin this discussion by exploring the question of whether war can ever be a good thing, because underlying this question are certain assumptions that require careful examination. Would it be a demonstration of goodness to show no opposition to evil? Can we approve of a government that stands by and offers no resistance to criminals, be they burglars, rapists, murderers, or child-abusers? Both the Old and New Testaments present a portrait of a God who judges evil. One of the means of God's judgment in the Old Testament is war. It is interesting to note that God's chosen people Israel are not always the ones who bring about God's will on the battlefield. In fact, they are often on the receiving end of his judgment, finding themselves massacred and enslaved just as, at other times, they are militarily victorious over other powers.

The rules of war for God's people are laid down in Deuteronomy 20, and they represent a control of justice, fairness and kindness in the use of the sword. Special hardship conditions were defined as grounds for excusing individual soldiers from military duty until those conditions were cleared up (Deuteronomy 20:5–7). Even those who had no such excuse but were simply afraid and reluctant to fight were likewise allowed to go home (verse 8). Unlike the contemporary armies of other nations, who might attack a city without giving it an opportunity to surrender on terms (cf. 1 Samuel 11:2–3; 20:1–2), the armies of Israel were required to grant a city a chance to capitulate without bloodshed before moving on to mount a full-scale siege and the destruction of the city. In this context the women and children were to be spared from death and were to be cared for by their captors (Deuteronomy 20:14). Only in the case of the particularly depraved inhabitants of Canaan itself was there to be total destruction. The reason given for this was the likely corruption of the moral and spiritual standards of Israelite society, in areas such as child sacrifice: 'they will teach you to follow all the detestable things they do in worshipping their gods, and you will sin against the LORD your God' (Deuteronomy 20:16–18). This is important, because Israel had been chosen to be the bearers of God's self-revelation to the world; they had been given the precious task of making God known.

Two different pictures of God?

Many people would pit the Old Testament picture of a 'violent God' who destroys his enemies on the battlefield against the New

Testament understanding of God as a God of love who sends his
Son to the cross to die for evil people.[1] In fact, Jesus actually tells
his disciples to 'Put your sword back in its place' (Matthew 26:52).
However, we do see the awesome, judging, powerful God who
destroys evil in the New Testament in such places as Revelation
20:11–15:

> Then I saw a great white throne and him who was seated
> on it. Earth and sky fled from his presence, and there was no
> place for them. And I saw the dead, great and small, standing
> before the throne, and books were opened. Another book
> was opened, which is the book of life. The dead were judged
> according to what they had done as recorded in the books.
> The sea gave up the dead that were in it, and death and
> Hades gave up the dead that were in them, and each person
> was judged according to what he had done. Then death and
> Hades were thrown into the lake of fire. The lake of fire is
> the second death. If anyone's name was not found written in
> the book of life, he was thrown into the lake of fire.

We need to take a big-picture view of war and struggle from the
beginning of the Bible to the end and see the whole as a cosmic
struggle between good and evil. As we have seen, a Christian
reading of the Old Testament would interpret the battles it depicts
in this context of a larger struggle. The battle of Jericho, the
wars against the southern coalition of Canaanite kings and the wars
against the northern coalition in Canaan would be included in this.
God fought on behalf of many of the judges in the Old Testament,
as well as faithful kings such as David and Jehoshaphat. In fact, at
times God used foreign nations to fight against Israel's enemies in a
way that helped his people. For example, the prophet Nahum
announced the appearance of the divine warrior who would fight
(in this instance through the Babylonians) against Israel's long-time
oppressor, Assyria.

It is crucial, as we try to take this big-picture view of a cosmic struggle, that we do not forget that God also used war against his own people to judge them. It would be a misunderstanding of the Old Testament to say that 'God was on Israel's side and that's all there is to it.' The fact that God had chosen Israel to be his people was not a *carte blanche* to wage war against anyone at any time. At certain times God used Israel as an instrument of his judgment against evil, oppressive nations. However, this raises the question of what would happen if Israel itself turned against God and committed evil acts.

The biblical context of any judgment against Israel is that God has made a treaty with his people. In this arrangement, Yahweh promises to be their God and protect them, and Israel promises to be his people and obey the law he has given them. Written into the covenant treaty between God and his people, there are certain consequences which will follow the working out of the treaty. Blessings flow from obedience and faithfulness to the promises made, and curses from disobedience. The book of Deuteronomy describes these blessings and curses in some detail. For example, obedience will have the following consequences:

> The LORD will grant that the enemies who rise up against you will be defeated before you. They will come at you from one direction but flee from you in seven.
> (28:7)

But disobedience will lead to these results:

> The LORD will cause you to be defeated before your enemies. You will come at them from one direction but flee from them in seven, and you will become a thing of horror to all the kingdoms on earth.
> (28:25)

There is a whole book of the Bible devoted to giving an emotional and theological response to the fall of Jerusalem – the book of

Lamentations. This book paints a picture of God as a warrior, but in this case the warrior is not protecting his people. In fact he is acting as their enemy:

> The Lord is like an enemy;
>   he has swallowed up Israel.
> He has swallowed up all her palaces
>   and destroyed her strongholds.
> He has multiplied mourning and lamentation
>   for the Daughter of Judah.
> (2:5)

The history of Israel has many examples of the outworking of these covenant curses, as well as the blessings. Commands from God to go into battle and kill people may seem to contradict the idea of a God of love, but the Christian interprets these passages in the context of the overall story of the Bible, which introduces us to a God who is just and good, who fights against evil and judges those who fight against him.

The coming of Christ and the beginning of the New Testament institutes a new era in a biblical understanding of battle. Jesus appears as the divine warrior, but he has intensified and heightened the battle. No longer is it a physical battle against flesh-and-blood enemies, but rather it is directed towards the spiritual powers and authorities.

The exorcisms of the New Testament point towards this. Here we see the violent nature of the conflict. In Matthew 8:28–34 (see also Mark 5:1–20; Luke 8:26–39) Jesus orders the demons in a possessed man to enter into some pigs, which then throw themselves into a lake and are destroyed. Jesus has authority over all the powers in the universe, even though they assert themselves against him. It is ultimately in his death on the cross that he demonstrates his supremacy over that which would oppose him. The apostle Paul looks back on the crucifixion and pronounces it a military victory over the demonic realm:

He forgave us all our sins, having cancelled the written code, with its regulations, that was against us and that stood opposed to us; he took it away, nailing it to the cross. And having disarmed the powers and authorities, he made a public spectacle of them, triumphing over them by the cross.
(Colossians 2:13–15)

Jesus' ascension into heaven is also described in military language, when Psalm 68 is referred to in Ephesians 4:7–8:

But to each one of us grace has been given as Christ apportioned it. This is why it says:

'When he ascended on high,
   he led captives in his train
   and gave gifts to men.'

Jesus defeated the powers and authorities, not by killing people but by dying for them. This transition – from the old way of thinking about the battle in terms of some kind of physical conflict, to the new era of spiritual warfare – was dramatically demonstrated when Jesus was arrested in the Garden of Gethsemane. The Gospels describe how Jesus' disciple Peter grabbed a sword and chopped off the ear of the high priest's servant (Matthew 26:47–56; Mark 14:43–52; Luke 22:47–53; John 18:1–11). Jesus responded by healing the man's ear and saying:

Put your sword back in its place . . . for all who draw the sword will die by the sword. Do you think I cannot call on my Father, and he will at once put at my disposal more than twelve legions of angels? But how then would the Scriptures be fulfilled that say it must happen in this way?
(Matthew 26:52–54)

The object of Christ's warfare is spiritual, not physical, and the weapons used are also spiritual. This becomes one of the most important metaphors for living the Christian life. Ephesians 6:10–18 is the famous passage which employs military metaphors for the spiritual task of following Christ and living a prayerful, godly life:

> Finally, be strong in the Lord and in his mighty power. Put on the full armour of God so that you can take your stand against the devil's schemes. For our struggle is not against flesh and blood, but against the rulers, against the authorities, against the powers of this dark world and against the spiritual forces of evil in the heavenly realms. Therefore put on the full armour of God, so that when the day of evil comes, you may be able to stand your ground, and after you have done everything, to stand. Stand firm then, with the belt of truth buckled round your waist, with the breastplate of righteousness in place, and with your feet fitted with the readiness that comes from the gospel of peace. In addition to all this, take up the shield of faith, with which you can extinguish all the flaming arrows of the evil one. Take the helmet of salvation and the sword of the Spirit, which is the word of God. And pray in the Spirit on all occasions with all kinds of prayers and requests. With this in mind, be alert and always keep on praying for all the saints.

There is therefore some discontinuity between the Old and New Testaments when it comes to warfare. While in the Old Testament war was often used by God as an instrument of his judgment, Jesus has shown that it is now a betrayal of the gospel to take up physical arms to defend or promote the interests of Christ. However, this discontinuity is not absolute.[2] There is also continuity, especially as we look to the New Testament's picture of the final judgment and its form of warfare, which uses spiritual weapons to demolish spiritual strongholds.

A Christian response to warfare

Having looked at the issue of war in the Old Testament and how that fits into an overall view of the Bible, the next question seems to be, What should a Christian response to physical warfare be? We have seen that the New Testament talks of the cosmic struggle between good and evil in spiritual terms, since the revelation of God through the physical nation of Israel has found ultimate fulfilment in the person of Christ. However, what has this all meant during the last two thousand years in terms of a Christian view of war?

The New Testament itself does not condemn the vocation of a soldier, if the work is carried out in a responsible and lawful fashion (Matthew 8:5; Luke 3:14; Acts 10:1–6, 34–35). And yet other passages seem to point towards pacifism: 'Blessed are the peace-makers, for they will be called sons of God' (Matthew 5:9).

There are, broadly, four Christian positions when it comes to seeking a biblical response to the concept of war. These are:

1. *Thoroughgoing militarism* – any war, anytime, any place, any cause.
2. *Selective militarism* – only when the state declares that the cause is just.
3. *Selective pacifism* – only when the individual thinks that the cause is just.
4. *Thoroughgoing pacifism* – no fighting anytime, any place, for any cause.[3]

Most Christians today would fall into the middle two. However, the early church's response to war was initially pacifism which allowed for the possibility of Christian converts staying on in the army. Pre-Constantinian theologians and church leaders such as Tertullian took the rebuke of Peter as an absolutist position that totally spiritualized the battles in the Old Testament and did not allow for any Christian approval of war. Origen was very concerned to show that Christians were not bad citizens by virtue of refusing to fight or kill. He developed an argument that Christian prayers would be of more use to the emperor than any amount of killing by soldiers.

It is the great theologian Augustine who introduces the fledgling 'just war' theory into Christian thinking. This theory originated in classical thinking, but Augustine built on this and the fourth-century theologian Ambrose developed it.[4]

Augustine begins by justifying some wars by the fact that God orders wars in the Old Testament. He frames (as does Aquinas) a deontological or ethical argument: If God allows and orders war in the Old Testament, then the nature of God as 'just' determines that there must be such a thing as a just war. God cannot order what is immoral. This is then the starting place for laying down principles by which a Christian can deduce whether or not a particular war is a 'just war'.

The development of just-war principles

Going to war (jus ad bellum)
The first set of principles deals with reasons for a nation going to war:

1. The war must be declared by a sovereign authority.
2. The cause must be just.
3. Those who fight must do so with the right intention of bringing about good and destroying evil.
4. War must be the last resort; all other methods for peaceful settlement through diplomacy must have been tried first.
5. The good achieved as a result of the war must outweigh the evil which led to the war.

Conduct of war (jus in bello)
The second set of principles deals with the *modus operandi* of a war:

1. Innocent civilians should not be killed.
2. The force used must be in proportion to the needs of the situation.

Most Protestant and Catholic churches adhere to these rules about war, and Scripture is clear that war is a disastrous tragedy in which the innocent always suffer, as well as the guilty. The psalmist laments war, and the prophet looks for the day when swords will be beaten into ploughshares and the kingdom of Shalom appears. The New Testament blesses peacemakers and Jesus resists being made King by force.

From beginning to end, the story of the Bible takes place in the context of a cosmic battle between good and evil which is introduced to us in Genesis and runs through until Revelation. At different moments in history this war takes different forms. As God's chosen people are commanded to enter the physical land which he gives them, they are ordered to displace the evil practices which have gone on there and must resist being drawn into these things themselves. This is because Israel is God's chosen means of self-revelation to the world, which will find its ultimate fulfilment in the person of Christ, who is born a Jew. Nothing must be allowed to corrupt this revelation of God to the world, and therefore some peoples are fought and destroyed. This happens at a moment in history but does not give a licence for any individuals or subsequent nations to go and do likewise. All of this must also be seen in the light of the reality that God raises up other nations' armies to come and judge Israel. They too experience the judgment of God against their sins.

When the New Testament comes, Jesus is the fulfilment of the promises and longings of the Old Testament. He is God come down to earth in human flesh. As the Bible puts it: 'In the past God spoke to our forefathers through the prophets at many times and in various ways, but in these last days he has spoken to us by his Son' (Hebrews 1:1–2).

Jesus conquers evil through his death on the cross and calls his followers to appropriate that victory in their own lives and to continue the spiritual battle through prayer and a life of service, following him. When wars occur between the nations of the world, Christians in different contexts must work out their involvement and reaction to those wars using biblical principles. The development of just-war theory by Christian thinkers of previous generations helps the contemporary church to do this in faithfulness to Christ and his Word.

9 Isn't the Bible out of date on sex?

One of the most highly charged objections to becoming a Christian is the strength of the moral challenge that the Bible presents. The change in lifestyle involved in following Christ may be daunting for many – particularly in the area of sexual ethics. It is also true to say that it is often over ethical issues that world-views collide. We may very well live alongside friends who have an entirely different belief system, and there may be little apparent difference in our lives, but when ethics become the topic of conversation, we will find that conflict and disagreement are not unusual.

The fact that the moral framework of the Bible is so counter-cultural in our twenty-first-century context means that moral questions feature prominently in the minds of non-Christians. I have experienced these questions coming time and time again. It is interesting that these are not often asked immediately, but as a conversation develops, the deeper questions of the heart are drawn out. It is even true to say that sometimes these sexual and moral issues provide the main foundation for a person not believing in God. Aldous Huxley wrote quite openly about his motivation for believing that life had no meaning and that there was no God:

> I had motives for not wanting the world to have a meaning; consequently I assumed that it had none and was able without any difficulty to find satisfying reasons for this assumption ... For myself as, no doubt, for most of my contemporaries, the philosophy of meaninglessness was essentially an instrument of liberation. The liberation we desired was simultaneously liberation from a certain political and economic system and liberation from a certain system of morality. We objected to the morality because it interfered with our sexual freedom; we objected to the political and economic system because it was unjust. The supporters of these systems claimed that in some way they embodied the meaning (a Christian meaning, they insisted) of the world. There was one admirably simple method in our political and erotic revolt: We could deny that the world had any meaning whatsoever.[1]

This is not to say that ethical objections to becoming a Christian are not real or heartfelt. I have met many students who have been close to becoming Christians who have asked, 'If I become a Christian do I have to stop sleeping with my boyfriend?' This is a real question which cuts to the heart of meaning and happiness. In other words: 'If I become a Christian do I have to give up the one thing in my life which brings me happiness?' Of course, we know that Jesus gives us life in abundance, that our salvation is not dependent on us working at moral purity but is a free gift. The Holy Spirit then helps us to follow Jesus and live lives that are morally pleasing to a holy God. But sometimes these questions raise doubts about the Bible. Can this book really be relevant or true if it says such apparently ridiculous things about sex?

Sex and marriage

We should probably start by looking at what the Bible actually says about sex before we decide whether or not this is out of date. It may come as a surprise that the biblical view of sex is extremely positive. God invented sex – he gave us this wonderful expression of love for another. There is a whole book of the Old Testament which is devoted to extolling the beauty of sex and showing God's delight in what he has made pleasurable and good.

The very beginning of the Bible lays a foundation for a Judaeo-Christian approach to sex. The early chapters of Genesis tell us that God created the first man and woman and, seeing what he had made, declared that it was 'very good'. Although the writer of Genesis does not go into detail about the distinctions between female and male, it is clear that each was an intentional creation and both were made in 'the image of God'. They were made not to be identical but to be complementary, and when the man sees the woman for the first time, he waxes lyrical about her otherness and sameness. She is clearly like him and unlike any other creature and yet she is intriguing and different – she is given to him as a companion and close partner. Genesis provides the original context for sexual intercourse and shows that God has designed this wonderful thing to be expressed within a life-long marital relationship between one man and one woman. Jesus earths his teaching on sexuality in these words, so clearly they are important.

The divine image is expressed in both male and female, and so the man and the woman are equally human despite their physical, anatomical and procreative differences. As they are joined together as husband and wife their unity and diversity is expressed: 'For this reason a man will leave his father and mother and be united to his wife, and they will become one flesh' (Genesis 2:24). Here we have a blueprint for human sexual love – through the sexual act the man and woman have a wonderful new kind of intimacy. This is called being 'one flesh', and it is designed to be exclusive and faithful.

Both Jesus and Paul pick up on this in the New Testament, emphasizing the beauty of monogamous marriage.

The biblical paradigm is not obsessed by sex and spends a good deal of time focusing on other kinds of loving relationship which function without a sexual element. We have brotherly and sisterly love, love expressed in close friendships – often between friends of the same sex. A well-known example of this is the close friendship of David and Jonathan in the Old Testament. Christ himself had close friends whom he spoke of on a par with family (Mark 3:33–35). He even had a best friend – the beloved disciple John (John 21:20). It is important in our society, which is saturated with sexual innuendo and camaraderie, that we remember the place of close friendships in which non-erotic love is expressed. In this context we can see that there are people in the Bible who abstain from sex and live a single life. Jesus lived this way and commended others who chose to do the same, whether they were born this way (impotent or possibly with a strong same-sex orientation), or they had been made that way by other people (castrated courtiers), or they had been called to renounce marriage 'because of the kingdom of heaven' (Matthew 19:12).

Homosexuality

The prominence of disagreement within the church on the issue of homosexuality has led to this question being increasingly important. Screaming headlines in our newspapers berate the church for being 'outdated' or 'homophobic'. Bishops are even quoted as calling traditionalists 'Nazis' and other such pejorative terms. This debate is often phrased in the context of the Bible and what it does or doesn't say.

The first challenge laid down by the gay lobby is that tradition-alists need to 'catch up' with modern culture. The Bible texts should be taken as coming from a particular cultural context which is completely irrelevant to a Western liberal society. In a society where homosexual partnerships are culturally acceptable these texts do not apply any more. This means that the church should 'catch up' with the moral developments of the society in which it finds itself.

The assumption behind this argument is that the Bible was written in a moral context equivalent to the Victorian era in Britain, when any sexual activity outside of marriage was frowned upon. However, this is simply not the case. Homosexuality was widely practised in the Roman empire as well as in the preceding Greek civilization. Homosexual partnership between an older man and a youth was often seen as an integral part of a young man's education. While some Roman writers may have protested against the sexual abuse of slaves, where there was consent on both sides homosexual practice was accepted. It was in this context of widespread homosexual activity that the New Testament was written. So it seems that these texts are not entirely culturally conditioned, for they actually propound a morality which is counter-cultural, a moral standard which does not come from the Graeco-Roman culture within which the text is written, but instead strongly challenges it. The New Testament provides a moral vision which is radically and powerfully different from the culture within which it is authored, and in so doing points to a morality beyond any particular time or culture.

The same is true of the Old Testament. The cultural context of the Canaanite and Assyrian civilizations around Israel was a general acceptance of homosexual practice, and yet passages such as Genesis 19:1–29 make it clear that, as well as a gross breach of hospitality, the sexual proclivities of the men of Sodom are condemned. This is echoed in the New Testament in 2 Peter 2:6–10 and Jude 7. Leviticus 18:22 and 20:13 also rule out homosexual practice as a lifestyle choice for those of the Hebrew religion. Whereas the Assyrians outlawed forcible same-sex intercourse and the Egyptians may have banned pederasty, Israel is alone in viewing homosexual activity as wrong *per se*.[2]

We have already touched on the idea of everything being a matter of interpretation, but it is the New Testament biblical texts about homosexuality which are particularly contentious and debated over the airwaves. The texts in question are Romans 1:26–27, 1 Corinthians 6:9 and 1 Timothy 1:10. But we need to begin with Jesus' statements about sexual purity. In Matthew 15:19 and Mark 7:21 he condemns *porneia*, meaning 'fornication' or 'sexual immorality'. This is a catch-all term which covers all kinds of sexual intercourse outside of marriage. Jesus, speaking as a Jew to his own people about sexual morality, would certainly have had in mind the moral teaching of the Old Testament, including its teaching about homosexuality.

Probably the most well-known passage about homosexuality in the New Testament comes in Romans 1:18–32. Paul's primary concern here is not homoerotic sexual practice but the more fundamental sin of not glorifying and giving thanks to God. Homosexual practice is presented as a symptom rather than a cause of this and comes in the context of a whole list of transgressions which dishonour God. Although this passage seems to be a clear statement that homosexuality is 'against nature', some have tried to argue that verse 26 seems to be referring to those who temporarily abandon their heterosexual inclination for fleeting homosexual experiences, rather than those whose orientation is homosexual.[3] The first problem with this is that the concept of 'homosexual orientation' would not have been recognizable to the author – it is a modern concept which is being read back into the text. In this context 'against nature', given as it is in a passage about different forms of idolatry which oppose God as Creator and his created order, is much more likely to mean 'against God's purpose for human creatures'.[4] Paul believed that God created man and woman and designed them for sexual relationship and procreation to take place in the context of marriage. Homosexual practice is one aspect of a distortion of that creation plan, and it is given here in the context of other practices which do this.

Paul, the apostle to the Gentile world, who would have come across homosexuality in his evangelism in the Roman empire, mentions it again in 1 Corinthians 6:9. Two words are used in the Greek to describe homosexual practice: *malakos*, which literally means 'soft'; and *arsenokoitai*, which literally means 'liers with males'. This latter word is a general term which seems to be based on the Hebrew term used in the Old Testament. Paul includes homosexual activity in a list of sins confirming that the church is made up of sinners, and no one sin is singled out for special condemnation. However, although members of the church may have struggled with these sins, they are not accepted as authentic Christian practices: 'And that is what some of you were. But you were washed, you were sanctified, you were justified in the name of the Lord Jesus Christ and by the Spirit of our God' (1 Corinthians 6:11). These things are wrong for the Christian, but many in the church have come out of this kind of background.

Again, in 1 Timothy 1:10 Paul rules out homosexual practice, using the word *arsenokoitai*. It is interesting that he uses this word when more precise words for different practices were available. This term is a general compound word which denotes a whole range of same-sex sexual activity.

Often the case for homosexuality as acceptable within Scripture is made by arguing that the Old Testament is superseded by the New Testament which focuses on love, inclusivity and acceptance. However, this is too simplistic. Protestant tradition has distinguished between the civil and ceremonial law of the Old Testament which applied to the historic nation of Israel and were fulfilled by Jesus, and the moral law which is an underlying code upheld by Christ. Where Christ does seem to draw a line under Old Testament law – for example, the civil penalty of stoning for adultery in John 8:1–11 – he upholds the moral law, telling the woman to 'Go now and leave your life of sin.' Of course, the distinctions between civil, ceremonial and moral law are not always clear, but it does seem to hold good as a general tool of interpretation. This, added to the general prohibition of same-sex activity for Christian believers given in the New Testament, presents a unified biblical message on this moral question.

And so we see that although both the Old and New Testaments were given in eras which found homosexual activity culturally and morally acceptable, the texts are counter-cultural and call for a different moral standard amongst believers from that of the world around. While recognizing that what the Bible says about homosexual practice may seem controversial and unpopular, it is important to remember that it would also have seemed so at the time it was written. So although the Bible may seem 'out of date', the culture in which it was written was not so dissimilar from our own.

It is also important to draw a distinction between 'homophobia' – an irrational hatred or hostility towards homosexual people – and a disapproval of homosexual practice for confessing Christians on biblical grounds. The Evangelical Alliance writes: 'We cannot however accept that to disapprove of homosexual practice on biblical grounds is in itself irrational, hateful or hostile.'[5] The tendency of the gay lobby to brand anyone who disagrees with their position as 'homophobic' is regrettable because it fails to consider the nuances of biblical interpretation and the consciences of Christian believers.

The next issue is the question of tolerance. An objection to taking what the Bible says on homosexuality at face value is that this would be extremely intolerant and would exclude diversity. However, it is interesting that passions run high on both sides of this debate. It would be naïve to suppose that one side is entirely inclusive and tolerant. The vehemence with which the gay lobby have pursued their aim of gaining acceptance for homosexual practice within the church is noteworthy. One churchman has called traditionalists 'Anglican Taliban'.[6] In an interview in the Italian newspaper *La Repubblica*, Cardninal Joseph Ratzinger described the development of a 'secular ideological aggression' across the continent of Europe as 'cause for concern'. He cited an example which is of interest to us here: 'In Sweden, a Protestant minister who preached about homosexuality on the basis of an excerpt from the scriptures was put in jail for a month.'[7] It is interesting that the Swedish pastor's views could not be tolerated.

The question is not so much who excludes somebody – traditionalists would exclude a pro-gay reading of the Bible and the gay lobby would exclude a traditionalist understanding. This brings us back to an important reality, which is that truth excludes its opposite. We should not reject the Bible and its message on the basis of the fact that some lifestyles or opinions may be excluded by what it says – because that very rejection of the Bible also itself excludes certain points of view, just different views.

While the practice of same-sex sexual activity is not an innovation by the Western liberal societies of the twentieth and twenty-first centuries, it appears that the view that some people are by 'nature' homosexual has entered mainstream opinion more recently. The question posed to the Bible may be something along these lines: 'How can a loving God deny people the opportunity to be what they are by nature?' While this 'essentialist' view can be traced back as far as Aristotle,[8] it has gained much ground through research conducted in the twentieth century and has emerged as a popular position today. Over the last century it has displaced 'constructionist' explanations which have attributed homosexual tendencies to social and environmental factors rather than genetic ones. However, it is not Christians alone who would dispute the idea that some people are gay by nature or that one's sexual orientation is in some way predetermined. It is interesting that Peter Tatchell, the vocal gay rights campaigner and the founder of 'Outrage!', has condemned any search for a 'gay gene' as 'the flawed theory which claims a genetic causation for homosexuality'.[9] It is likely that a whole range of factors contribute to a homosexual orientation, from environmental conditions to hormonal or behavioural ones. The human being still has a capacity to make choices and pursue goals. The Christian would want to affirm the dignity of every human being and make a distinction between personhood and behaviour. This is why it is possible for a Christian to say that homosexual activity is wrong, but people who have a homo-sexual orientation are loved and welcomed. For a Christian, identity does not come from what I do, whether that be vocational or sexual; my identity is rooted in being a child of God. What I do then flows from that.

The role of choice in our sexual behaviour cannot be over-stated. Although our inclination may lead us in a certain direction, we still have a choice about what we do with that. However we define our orientation, we must take responsibility for our actions. As one writer puts it:

> Distinguishing between homosexual orientation and homoerotic sexual practice leaves open the question of whether orientation relates primarily to genetics, or whether it has predominantly social or environmental causation. Neither does such a distinction compel us to regard homosexuality as an entirely fixed 'condition' which must inevitably determine someone's identity and sexual behaviour.[10]

Some recent British research concludes that 'exclusively homo-sexual behaviour appears to be rare' and 'homosexual experience is often a relatively isolated or passing event' in people's lives.[11] This seems to be supported by a controversial piece of research published by Dr Robert Spitzer, professor of psychiatry at Columbia University, New York. He is well known for having been instrumental in deleting homosexuality from the American Psychiatric Association's list of mental disorders in 1973. His recent study has caused uproar by suggesting that homosexuals can change their sexuality. He found that 78% of males and 95% of females who voluntarily underwent 'reparative' or psychiatric therapy reported a change in their sexuality. Of the 143 men and 57 women who participated, 66% of males and 44% of females had achieved what he called 'good heterosexual func-tioning'. This study has been vociferously criticized because many of the participants expressed the fact that their Christian faith had helped them. The research has been decried as 'fundamentalist' and 'bogus'. However, Dr Spitzer describes himself as an 'atheist Jew' whose interest is in scientific truth. He writes:

> My conclusion is that the door is open ... I came to this study as a sceptic – I believed that a homosexual, whether born or made, was a homosexual and that to consider their orientation a matter of choice was wrong. But the fact is that if I found even one person who could change, the door is open, and a change in sexual orientation is possible.[12]

Whether or not one's sexual orientation is a fixed, unchangeable fact (and this is certainly open to question), the important thing for the Christian is that our sexuality does not completely define our identity. The God of the Bible loves every human being – we are all made in his image, and his offer of forgiveness and new life is open to all.

This means that the most important thing for the Christian is not to decide whether someone's sexual orientation is genetic or acquired, nor whether it is constant or fluid, but to deal with the question of behaviour. The Bible lays down teaching on how those who wish to follow Christ and 'enter the kingdom of heaven' should behave. This touches on all kinds of areas of life, one of which is our sexual behaviour. Our decision then, once we have become Christians, is to try to live in obedience to these standards. This will not always be easy. Many of our inclinations may try to lead us away from God's standard, but this does not mean that the teaching of the Bible changes.

10 How can I know?

We have looked at some of the tough questions asked of the Bible and examined some of the reasons why these objections might be raised. In this final chapter we come to an important point which has to do with personalizing some of what has been said. Is it actually possible to 'know' what is true? Perhaps some objections or barriers in the way of belief have been removed, but still we are not actually sure. This is an interesting phenomenon and it brings us to one of the most important realities of the Christian faith. Whatever intellectual facts an individual may or may not accept, this does not necessarily mean that person knows God. The heart of the Christian faith is the revelation of a personal God, who can be known and related to.

Now, it may be that you don't even believe that God exists. Let me encourage you to be open to the possibility that he does. As for the atheist who is certain that God does not exist, I would ask you to think about whether it is really possible to prove an absolute negation. What do I mean by that? Imagine we were talking about the existence of green spotted stones in the universe today instead of God. What would I have to do to prove that green spotted stones do not exist? I would have to have an exhaustive knowledge of the universe, an absolute knowledge – that would make me God. What do I have to do to say that green spotted stones do exist? – Find one. Let me encourage you to at least be open to the existence of God.

My own story is one of knowing God in a personal way. I know some facts about Jesus, but there is more to it than that – I actually know Jesus personally. I was born in Australia where my parents had emigrated so that my father could take up a position at the University of New South Wales, teaching Politics. My parents are both true intellectuals, valuing discussion and debate of literature, the arts, politics and just about anything else. However, in their early thirties they came to a point in life where they seemed to have everything they had pursued, and they began to question the ultimate meaning of life. My father went along to various spiritual groups of different flavours, but was surprised at one meeting to hear a Christian say: 'The only reason you should accept Christianity is because it is true ...' He found this rather a startling remark coming from a religious person, but went on with his life as it was. Then one night, as he was marking some students' papers alone in his study, he had an experience of God. He saw all kinds of different situations in his life where he had hurt others or acted selfishly, and then saw the reaction of Jesus to those things. He then found himself seeing the cross and kneeling before it. He had been raised by an atheist father who had forbidden churchgoing, but the words of Scripture, 'Lord, I believe; help my unbelief' came into his mind, so he said them. He found himself experiencing the love and forgiveness of Jesus and, overwhelmed, went into the bedroom to wake up my mother. He woke her up with the words, 'Jane, the most fantastic thing has happened – I have become a Christian!' She rolled over, decidedly underwhelmed by this, and went back to sleep. A few days after becoming a Christian my father thought to himself: 'How could I meet others who have had a similar experience?' It slowly dawned that church might be a place to find other believers in Jesus. However, he was reluctant to go alone and persuaded my mother to accompany him. She had gone to a British boarding school in the 1960s and had experienced a dreary Church of England service every day at school, which had acted as an effective inoculation against religion. But she thought to herself: 'I know my husband is an intelligent man – I know how to get him out of this Christian phase.' So she said, 'I will only come if it is an Anglican church,' thinking, 'This will cure him for life!' Through the Yellow Pages they found a nearby church and went along on a Sunday. It was a Bible-believing, lively church and my father loved it. My mother detested it – she had not yet discovered the reality of God for herself. This came about six months later, after much questioning and searching. Because of this I was raised in a home in which God was real and active. I read the Bible every day and completed my first cover-to-cover reading of it by about the age of six. I heard brilliant, lively and thoughtful sermons about the Bible every week (my father became a minister), and I experienced a relationship with Jesus from a young age. I saw prayers answered and miracles occurring.

Now, of course, some people would argue that I was conditioned and raised to believe in God and the Bible, and so I do. But let me ask you: 'Were you raised in a home that was entirely value-free, completely neutral about all beliefs?' Of course not – we are all raised in an environment which influences our thinking, values and behaviour. None of us is completely conditioned by that – in fact, the popular joke about vicars' daughters being the most raucous non-Christians anyone can meet demonstrates this! We grow up, begin to question and make our own way in the world. I went on to study theology at Oxford – often a sure-fire way of losing any childhood faith.

In fact, I still vividly remember being asked at my Oxford interview: 'You are only eighteen – what will you do when you come to Oxford and realize that everything you believe is wrong and your naïve evangelical views about the Bible come crashing down?' Note the neutral, unbiased perspective of the question! I answered that I was confident that what I believed was true and real – and if this was the case, it ought to be able to stand up to scrutiny and questions. The questions have come and gone, some have been harder than others, but eventually I have found satisfying answers that make me conclude that the Christian world-view gives us the most plausible explanation of reality. It describes and diagnoses the concerns of the universe, but it does more than this – Jesus actually deals with them.

This is where we come to the heart of the matter – God is a real, personal being, revealed to us in the person of Christ. Whatever questions or arguments we may have, in the end it all comes down to whether this is the case. Is Jesus real, can I know him? Can he really deliver me from my own sin?

The unique thing about Christian faith is that it is all about revelation. We as humans are not trying to work things out for ourselves, we do not have to follow a set of spiritual laws to gain enlightenment. God is the initiator – he reveals himself to us. Revelation means that communication actually occurs, the initiator is made known to a person. The Christian doctrine of the incarnation means that Jesus – through whom the universe came into existence, Jesus the first uncaused cause of the universe, Jesus who is God – enters space-time and history. He comes and walks on the earth, making God known as personal and real. God does not write a message about himself in the sky, send down a book of wisdom, or give individuals trances about himself. He actually comes to earth and makes himself personally knowable to human beings.

We can know this Jesus today. He died a gruesome death by crucifixion, but three days later he physically rose from the grave he was placed in. Now he says to us:

Here I am! I stand at the door [this means the door of our hearts] and knock. If anyone hears my voice and opens the door, I will come in and eat with him, and he with me. (Revelation 3:20)

It is my prayer that you will do this for yourself. Jesus promises that he will make himself known to those who seek after him.

Notes

Chapter 1: Isn't it all a matter of interpretation?

1. Sean Burke, *The Death and Return of the Author: Criticism and Subjectivity in Barthes, Foucault and Derrida* (Edinburgh, Edinburgh University Press, 1998).
2. Friedrich Nietzsche, *Twilight of the Idols*, translated by R. J. Hollingdale (Middlesex, Penguin Books, 1972).
3. Bertrand Russell is said to have quipped.
4. Ludwig Wittgenstein, *Philosophical Investigations*, 1.65 translated by G. E. M. Anscombe (Oxford, Basil Blackwell, 1935), pp. 32ff.
5. Jean-François Lyotard, *The Postmodern Condition: A Report on Knowledge*, translated by Geoff Benington and Brian Massumi (Minneapolis, University of Minnesota Press, 1984), p. 82.
6. Allan Megill, *Prophets of Extremity: Nietzsche, Heidegger, Foucault, Derrida* (London, University of California Press, 1987), p. 211.
7. Foucault, 'The Archaeology of Knowledge' and 'The Order of Discourse' in *Untying the Text: A Post-Structuralist Reader*, edited by Robert Young (London, Routledge, 1981).
8. Foucault, *Discipline and Punish: The Birth of the Prison*, translated by Alan Sheridan (New York, Vintage Books, 1977), p. 27.
9. Foucault, 'Truth and Power' in *Power/Knowledge: Selected Interviews and Other Writings, 1972–1977*, translated by Colin Gordon, Leo Marshall, John Mepham and Kate Soper (New York, Pantheon Books, 1980), p. 133.
10. Jacques Derrida, *Of Grammatology*, translated by Gayatri Chakravorty Spivak (Baltimore and London, John Hopkins University Press, 1998), p. 49.

Chapter 2: Can we know anything about history?

1. David Bowie quoted in *Sunday Times* magazine, 25 Sept. 1999.
2. E. P. Sanders in *The Spectator*, 6 Apr. 1996.
3. Greg Dening, *Mr Bligh's Bad Language: Passion, Power and Theatre on the Bounty* (Cambridge, Cambridge University Press, 1992), p. 366.
4. Foucault, 'Nietzsche, Genealogy, History' in Stanley Grenz, *A Primer on Postmodernism* (Michigan, Eerdmans, 1996), p. 131.
5. Michael Shermer and Alex Grobman, *Denying History* (London, University of California Press, 2000), p. 19.
6. D. D. Eisenhower, *Crusade in Europe* (New York, Doubleday, 1948), p. 409.

Chapter 3: Are the biblical manuscripts reliable?

1. *The Times*, quoted on website <http://www.soon.org.uk/page19.htm>.
2. John Warwick Montgomery, *History and Christianity* (Downers Grove, InterVarsity Press, 1973), p. 29.
3. Sir Frederic G. Kenyon, *Handbook to the Textual Criticism of the New Testament* (London, Macmillan, 1901), p. 4.
4. Ralph Earle, Merrill Unger and Millar Burrows, quoted by Josh McDowell, *The New Evidence that Demands a Verdict* (Nashville, Thomas Nelson, 1999), pp. 77–81.
5. Ibid.

Chapter 4: Is the content of the manuscripts reliable?

1. David Hume, *An Inquiry Concerning Human Understanding*, edited by Charles W. Hendel (New York, Liberal Arts, 1955), p. 173.
2. Norman L. Geisler, *Baker Encyclopaedia of Apologetics* (Grand Rapids, Baker Books, 1999), p. 341.
3. C. S. Lewis, *Miracles* (London and Glasgow, Collins Clear-Type Press, 1947), pp. 18–19.

4. Professor Richard Lewontin, 'Billions and Billions of Demons', *The New York Review*, 9 Jan. 1997, quoted in Joe Boot, *A Time to Search* (Eastbourne, Kingsway, 2002), p. 64.

5. *The Gospel According to Thomas*, Coptic text established and translated by A. Guillaumont, H.-Ch. Puech, G. Quispel, W. Till and Yassah 'Abd Al Masih (Leiden, Brill, 2001).

6. Flavius Josephus, *The Antiquities of the Jews* (New York, Ward, Lock, Bowden, 1900), 18.3.

7. Julius Africanus in F. F. Bruce, *The New Testament Documents: Are they Reliable?* (Leicester, IVP, 1964), p. 113.

8. Cornelius Tacitus, *Annals: Book 15*, edited by N. Miller (Bristol, Bristol Classical Press Latin Texts, 1998), p. 44.

9. Suetonius, *Life of Nero* in Josh McDowell, *The New Evidence that Demands a Verdict* (Nashville, Thomas Nelson, 1999), p. 121.

10. Suetonius, *Life of Claudius* in Josh McDowell, *The New Evidence that Demands a Verdict* (Nashville, Thomas Nelson, 1999), p. 121.

11. Pliny the Younger, *Letters*, Book 10, Harvard Classics Series, translated by William Melmoth (New York, Collier and Son, 1909–14), Letter 96.

12. Norman L. Geisler and William E. Nix, *A General Introduction to the Bible* (Chicago, Moody Press, 1986), p. 408.

13. These rules reveal an astounding reverence for the scriptural text:

1. A synagogue roll must be written on the skins of clean animals.
2. It must be prepared for the particular use of the synagogue by a Jew.
3. The rolls must be fastened together with strings taken from clean animals.
4. Every skin must contain a certain number of columns, equal throughout the entire codex.

5. The length of each codex must not extend over less than 48 lines or more than 60 lines; and the breadth must consist of 30 letters.

6. The whole copy must first be lined, and if three words are written without a line the whole thing is worthless.

7. The ink must be black – not red nor green nor any other colour, and it must be prepared according to a definite recipe.

8. An authentic copy must be the exemplar, from which the transcriber must not deviate.

9. No word or letter, not even a yod, must be written from memory, the scribe not having looked at the codex before him.

10. Between every consonant the space of a hair or thread must intervene.

11. Between every section there must be a space the breadth of nine consonants.

12. Between every book there must be a space of three lines.

13. The fifth book of the Pentateuch must terminate exactly with a line, but the rest need not do so.

14. The copyist must sit in full Jewish dress.

15. He must wash his whole body.

16. He must not begin to write the name of God with a pen newly dipped in ink.

17. And should a king address him while he is writing that name, he must take no notice of him.

(From Samuel Davidson, *The Hebrew Text of the Old Testament* [London, 1856], p. 89.)

14. F. F. Bruce, *The Books and Parchments: How we got our English Bible* (Basingstoke, Pickering and Inglis, 1984), p. 117.

Chapter 5: What about the canon?

1. Alister McGrath, *Christian Theology: An Introduction*, (Oxford, Blackwells, 2001), pp. 13–14.

2. Justin Martyr, *The First Apology of Justin Martyr, Addressed to the Emperor Antoninus Pius* (London, Griffith Farran Okeden and Welsh, 1891), 1.67.
3. John Barton, *How the Bible Came to Be* (Westminster, John Knox Press, 1998), p. 85.
4. Athanasius, L 552, quoted in Josh McDowell, *The New Evidence that Demands a Verdict* (Nashville, Thomas Nelson, 1999), p. 24.
5. F. F. Bruce, *The Books and Parchments: How we got our English Bible* (Basingstoke, Pickering and Inglis, 1984), p. 117.
6. Jerome, quoted in Norman L. Geisler and William E. Nix, *A General Introduction to the Bible* (Chicago, Moody Press, 1986), pp. 272–273.

Chapter 6: What about the other holy books?
1. Steve Turner, 'The Atheist's Creed' in *The King of Twist* (London, Hodder & Stoughton Religious, 1992).
2. The world's two largest standing Buddha statues, which had been carved in the sandstone cliffs of Bamiyan City 1,700 years ago, were blown up with dynamite on 12 March 2001.
3. Quoted in Annemarie Schimmel, *And Muhammad is His Messenger* (Chapel Hill and London, University of North Carolina Press, 1985), p. 62.
4. See Chapter 3 on the manuscripts.
5. Al-Bukhari, *The Translation of the Meaning of Sahih Al-Bukhari*, translated by Muhammad Muhshin Khan (al-Medina, Islamic University, 1983), vol. 6, pp. 477–478.
6. Ibid., pp. 478–479.
7. *Atlantic Monthly*, Jan. 1999. Andrew Rippon is Professor of Religious Studies at Calgary University, Canada.
8. Sayyid Hossein Nasr, *Ideals and Realities of Islam* (London, George Allen & Unwin, 1966; Boston, Beacon Press, 1966), p. 47.
9. See Andrew Rippon, *Muslims: Their Religious Beliefs and Practices*, Vol. 1 (London, Routledge, 1990). pp. 59–73 for

a good introduction to the development of Qur'anic interpretations.

10. The four *Samhitas* are: *Rig Veda* (Veda of hymns or verses); *Yajur-Veda* (Veda of rituals); *Sama-Veda* (Veda of melodies); and *Atharva-Veda* (Veda of incantations and spells).

11. F. M. Muller (1823–1900) is called the founder of the discipline of comparative religion. He did ground-breaking work in Oxford, translating Hindu sacred texts and writing critical academic books in this field. It was Muller who first proposed the chronology of the Aryan invasion of India, which most Western scholars of Hinduism broadly work within.

12. *The Complete Works of Swami Vivekananda* (Calcutta, Advaita Ashrama, 10th ed., 1963), vol. 1, p. 438.

13. P. Olivelle, *Upanisads Translated from the Original Sanskrit* (Oxford, Oxford University Press, 1996), p. 36.

Chapter 7: Isn't the Bible sexist?

1. R. Eliezer (c. AD 80–120), *The Mishnah*, translated and edited by H. Danby (Oxford, Oxford University Press, 1980), p. 296.

2. C. E. B. Cranfield and William Sanday, *Romans: Chapters 9 – 16 & Essays, International Critical Commentary*, Vol. 2 (Edinburgh, Continuum International Publishing Group, 1979).

3. Leonard Swidler, *Biblical Affirmations of Woman* (Philadelphia, Westminster Press, 1979), p. 310.

4. Henry George Liddell and R. Scott, *Greek-English Lexicon*, 9th ed. (Oxford, Oxford University Press, 1940).

5. Kenneth Bailey, 'Women in the New Testament', unpublished article, p. 6.

6. Chrysostom, *Homilies on Romans*, 31 NPNF, in P. Schaff et al., eds., *A Select Library of the Nicene and Post-Nicene Fathers of the Christian Church* (Peabody, Mass., Hendrickson, reprint 1994), 1 11:554–555.

7. Bernadette J. Brooten, *Women Leaders in the Ancient Synagogue: Inscriptional Evidence and Background Issues* (Atlanta, Scholars Press, 1982), p. 141.

8. James Dunn, *Word Biblical Commentary: Romans 9 – 16* (Carlisle, Paternoster Press, 1988), and Douglas Moo, *New International Commentary on the New Testament: Epistle to the Romans* (Michigan, W. B. Eerdmans, 1996), p. 922.

9. Kenneth Bailey, 'Women in the New Testament', unpublished article.

10. Clarence J. Vos, *Women in Old Testament Worship* (Delft, N. V. Verenge Drukkerijen Judels & Brinkman, 1968), p. 168.

Chapter 8: What about all the wars?

1. P. Craigie, *The Problem of War in the Old Testament* (Grand Rapids, MI, Eerdmans, 1978); M. Lind, *Yahweh is a Warrior. The Theology of Warfare in Ancient Israel* (Scottsdale, PA, Herald, 1980); P. D. Miller, *The Divine Warrior in Early Israel* (Cambridge, MA, Harvard University, 1973); S. Niditch, *War in the Hebrew Bible. A Study in the Ethics of Violence* (New York, Orbis, 1992); G. Von Rad, *Holy War in Ancient Israel* (Grand Rapids, MI, Eerdmans, 1991); J. G. Williams, *The Bible, Violence, and the Sacred. Liberation from the Myths of Sanctioned Violence* (San Francisco, Harper & Row, 1991).

2. For further study on this, see Stanley N. Gundry, ed., *Show Them No Mercy: 4 Views on God and the Canaanite Genocide* (Grand Rapids, Zondervan, 2003).

3. Robin Gill, *A Textbook of Christian Ethics* (London, T. & T. Clark, 2002), pp. 257ff.

4. Aquinas systematized the theory in the thirteenth century, and Francisco de Vitari developed it in the sixteenth century.

Chapter 9: Isn't the Bible out of date on sex?

1. Aldous Huxley, *Ends and Means* (London, Chatto & Windus, 1946), pp. 270–273.

2. Evangelical Alliance, *Faith, Hope and Homosexuality* (Carlisle, Paternoster Press, 1998), p. 17.

3. John Boswell, *Christianity, Social Tolerance and Homosexuality: Gay People in Western Europe from the Beginning of the Christian Era to the 14th Century* (Chicago, University of Chicago Press, 1981), p. 109.

4. Evangelical Alliance, *Faith, Hope and Homosexuality* (Carlisle, Paternoster Press, 1998), p. 18.

5. Ibid., p. 6.

6. Colin Slee, see <http://www.st-francis-lutheran.org/independo30713.html>.

7. *Daily Telegraph*, 20 Nov. 2004.

8. D. F. Greenberg, *The Construction of Homosexuality* (Chicago, University of Chicago Press, 1990), p. 404.

9. *The Times*, 20 Feb. 1997.

10. Evangelical Alliance, *Faith, Hope and Homosexuality* (Carlisle, Paternoster Press, 1998), p. 23.

11. Kaye Wellings, et al., *Sexual Behaviour in Britain: The National Survey of Sexual Attitudes and Lifestyles* (Middlesex, Penguin Books, 1994), pp. 203–213.

12. *Daily Telegraph*, 12 Oct. 2003.

Bibliography

Anderson, Norman, *Christianity and World Religions* (Leicester, IVP, 1984).

Barton, John, *How the Bible Came to Be* (Westminster, John Knox Press, 1998).

Blomberg, Craig, *The Historical Reliability of the Gospels* (Leicester, IVP, 1987).

Boswell, John, *Christianity, Social Tolerance and Homosexuality: Gay People in Western Europe from the Beginning of the Christian Era to the 14th Century* (Chicago, University of Chicago Press, 1981).

Brooten, Bernadette J., *Women Leaders in the Ancient Synagogue: Inscriptional Evidence and Background Issues* (Atlanta, Scholars Press, 1982).

Bruce, F. F., *The New Testament Documents: Are They Reliable?* (Leicester, IVP, 1964).

Bruce, F. F., *The Books and Parchments: How We Got Our English Bible* (Basingstoke, Pickering and Inglis, 1984).

Bunnett, David G., *The Spirit of Hinduism* (UK, Monarch Publications, 1992).

Chapman, Colin, *The Cross and the Crescent* (Leicester, IVP, 2002).

Clark, David K. & Geisler, Norman L., *Apologetics in the New Age: A Christian Critique of Pantheism* (USA, Baker Book House, 1990).

Cotterell, Peter & Riddell, Peter, *Islam in Conflict* (Leicester, IVP, 2003).

Cragie, P., *The Problem of War in the Old Testament* (Grand Rapids, Eerdmans, 1978).

Davidson, Samuel, *The Hebrew Text of the Old Testament* (London, 1856).

Evangelical Alliance, *Faith, Hope and Homosexuality* (Carlisle, Paternoster Press, 1998).

Geisler, Norman L., *False Gods of Our Time* (USA, Harvest House, 1985).

Geisler, Norman L., *Baker Encyclopaedia of Apologetics* (Grand Rapids, Baker Books, 1999).

Geisler, Norman L. & Nix, William E., *A General Introduction to the Bible* (Chicago, Moody Press, 1986).

Gill, Robin, *A Textbook of Christian Ethics* (London, T. & T. Clark, 2002).

Greenberg, D. F., *The Construction of Homosexuality* (Chicago, University of Chicago Press, 1990).

Groothuis, Douglas R., *Unmasking the New Age* (USA, InterVarsity Press, 1986).

Groothuis, Douglas R., *Confronting the New Age* (InterVarsity Press, 1988).

Groothuis, Douglas R., *Revealing the New Age Jesus* (USA, InterVarsity Press, 1990).

Gundry, Stanley N., ed., *Show Them No Mercy: Four Views on God and the Canaanite Genocide* (Grand Rapids, Zondervan, 2003).

Honeysett, Marcus, *Meltdown* (Leicester, IVP, 2002).

Humphreys, Christmas, *The Buddhist Way of Life* (India, Indus, 1980).

Johnson, David L., *A Reasoned Look at Asian Religions* (USA, Bethany House Publishers, 1985).

Kaiser, W., *The Old Testament Documents* (Leicester, IVP, 2001).

Kenyon, Sir Frderick G., *Handbook to the Textual Criticism of the New Testament* (London, Macmillan, 1901).

Langley, Myrtle, *World Religions* (Malaysia, Lion Publishing, 1993).

Lewis, C. S., *Miracles* (London & Glasgow, Collins Clear-Type Press, 1947).

Lind, M., *Yahweh is a Warrior: The Theology of Warfare in Ancient Israel* (Scottsdale, Herald, 1980).

Mangalwadi, Vishal, *When the New Age Gets Old* (USA, InterVarsity Press, 1992).

McCloughry, Roy, *Living in the Presence of the Future* (Leicester, IVP, 2001).

McDowell, Josh, *The New Evidence That Demands a Verdict* (Nashville, Thomas Nelson, 1999).

McDowell, Josh & Stewart, Don, *Concise Guide to Today's Religions* (UK, Scripture Press Foundation, 1990).

McGrath, Alister, *Explaining Your Faith* (Leicester, IVP, 1995).

McGrath, Alister, *Christian Theology: An Introduction* (Oxford, Blackwells, 2001).

Miller, Elliot, *A Crash Course on the New Age Movement* (USA, Baker Book House, 1993).

Miller, P. D., *The Divine Warrior in Early Israel* (Cambridge, MA, Harvard University, 1973).

Montgomery, John Warwick, *History and Christianity* (Downers Grove, InterVarsity Press, 1973).

Moucarry, Chawcat, *Faith to Faith* (Leicester, IVP, 2001).

Nasr, Sayyid Hossein, *Ideals and Realities of Islam* (London, George Allen & Unwin, 1966; Boston, Beacon Press, 1966).

Netland, H. A., *Encountering Religious Pluralism* (Leicester, Apollos, 2002).

Niditch, S., *War in the Hebrew Bible: A Study in the Ethics of Violence* (New York, Orbis, 1992).

Ramachandra, Vinoth, *Faiths in Conflict?* (Leicester, IVP, 1999).

Reisser, Paul C., Reisser, Teri K. & Weldon, John, *New Age Medicine* (USA, InterVarsity Press, 1987).

Riddell, Peter, *Christians and Muslims* (Leicester, IVP, 2004).

Rippon, Andrew, *Muslims: Their Religious Beliefs and Practices, Vol. 1* (London, Routledge, 1990).

Sampson, Philip, *Six Modern Myths* (Leicester, IVP, 2000).

Swidler, Leonard, *Biblical Affirmations of Woman* (Philadelphia, Westminster Press, 1979).

Turner, Steve, *The King of Twist* (London, Hodder & Stoughton Religious, 1992).

Van Leeuwen, Mary, *Fathers and Sons* (Leicester, IVP, 2002).

Vanhoozer, K. J., *Is There a Meaning in This Text?* (Leicester, Apollos, 1998).

Von Rad, G., *Holy War in Ancient Israel* (Grand Rapids, Eerdmans, 1991).

Vos, Clarence J., *Women in Old Testament Worship* (Delft, N. V. Verenge Drukkerijen Judels & Brinkman, 1968).

Wellings, Kaye, et al., *Sexual Behaviour in Britain: The National Survey of Sexual Attitudes and Lifestyles* (Middlesex, Penguin Books, 1994).

Williams, J. G., *The Bible, Violence, and the Sacred: Liberation from the Myths of Sanctioned Violence* (San Francisco, Harper & Row, 1991).